SMP interact

Higher
1
practice

for **AQA, Edexcel** and **OCR two-tier GCSE mathematics**

CAMBRIDGE
UNIVERSITY PRESS

The School Mathematics Project

Writing and editing for this edition John Ling, Paul Scruton, Susan Shilton, Heather West
SMP design and administration Melanie Bull, Pam Keetch, Nicky Lake, Cathy Syred, Ann White

The following people contributed to the original edition of SMP Interact for GCSE.

Benjamin Alldred	David Cassell	Spencer Instone	Susan Shilton
Juliette Baldwin	Ian Edney	Pamela Leon	Caroline Starkey
Simon Baxter	Stephen Feller	John Ling	Liz Stewart
Gill Beeney	Rosemary Flower	Carole Martin	Biff Vernon
Roger Beeney	John Gardiner	Lorna Mulhern	Jo Waddingham
Roger Bentote	Colin Goldsmith	Mary Pardoe	Nigel Webb
Sue Briggs	Bob Hartman	Paul Scruton	Heather West

CAMBRIDGE UNIVERSITY PRESS
Cambridge, New York, Melbourne, Madrid, Cape Town, Singapore, São Paulo

Cambridge University Press
The Edinburgh Building, Cambridge CB2 8RU, UK

www.cambridge.org
Information on this title: www.cambridge.org/9780521689977

© The School Mathematics Project 2007

First published 2007

Printed in the United Kingdom at the University Press, Cambridge

A catalogue record for this publication is available from the British Library

ISBN 978-0-521-68997-7 paperback

Typesetting and technical illustrations by The School Mathematics Project
Other illustrations by Chris Evans
Cover design by Angela Ashton
Cover image by Jim Wehtje/Photodisc Green/Getty Images

Using this booklet

This booklet, *Higher 1 practice*, provides well graded exercises on topics in the Higher tier up to about the level of GCSE grade B. The exercises can be used for homework, consolidation work in class or revision. They follow the chapters and sections of the *Higher 1* students' book, so where that is the text used for teaching, the planning of homework or extra practice is easy.

Even when some other teaching text is used, this booklet's varied and thorough material is ideal for extra practice: the section headings – set out in the detailed contents list on the next few pages – clearly describe the GCSE topics covered and can be related to all boards' linear and major modular specifications by using the cross-references that can be downloaded as Excel files from **www.smpmaths.org.uk**

It is sometimes appropriate to have a single practice exercise that covers two sections within a *Higher 1* chapter. Such sections are bracketed together in this booklet's contents list.

Sections in *Higher 1* that do not have corresponding practice in this booklet are shown ghosted in the contents list.

To help users identify material that can be omitted by some students – or just dipped into for revision or to check competence – sections estimated to be at national curriculum level 6 are marked as such in the contents list and as they occur in the booklet.

Marked with a red page edge at intervals through the booklet, there are sections of mixed practice on previous work; these are in corresponding positions to the reviews in the students' book.

 Questions to be done without a calculator are marked with this symbol.

Questions marked with a star are more challenging.

Answers to this booklet are downloadable from **www.smpmaths.org.uk** in PDF format.

Contents

1 Triangles and polygons 7
- A Special triangles and quadrilaterals level 6 7
- B Angles of a triangle level 6 7
- C Angles of a polygon level 6 8
- D Mixed questions 8

2 Drawing and using quadratic graphs 9
- A Parabolas and quadratic functions 9
- B Using graphs to solve problems 11

3 Distributions and averages 12
- A Review: mean, median, range and mode level 6 12
  (including stem-and-leaf tables)
- B Grouped frequencies level 6
- C Choosing class intervals level 6 14
- D Estimating a mean using mid-interval values 15
- E Frequency polygons 16

4 Fractions 17
- A Review: adding, subtracting and multiplying
- B Reciprocals 17
- C Dividing by a fraction 17
- D Mixed questions 17

5 Accuracy 18
- A Lower and upper bounds 18

6 Linear equations 1 19
- A Solving equations 19
- B Forming equations 19
- C Equations that involve a fraction
- D More than one fraction 21
- E Mixed questions

7 Area and perimeter 22
- A Parallelogram level 6 22
- B Triangle level 6 22
- C Composite shapes and algebra 23
- D Trapezium level 6 24
- E Circle 24
- F Population density 25
- G Converting units of area 26
- H Mixed questions 26

8 Percentages 27
- A Review: percentage change 27
- B Successive percentage changes 27
- C Compound interest 28
- D Percentage change in reverse 28
- E Mixed questions 29

Mixed practice 1 30

9 Transformations 32
- A Reflection level 6
- B Translation level 6 32
- C Rotation 33
- D Enlargement 33
- E Mixed questions 34

10 Powers and indices 35
- A Calculating with powers 35
- B Multiplying powers
- C Multiplying expressions with powers 36
- D Dividing powers
- E Dividing expressions with powers 37
- F Negative indices 38
- G Extending the rules to negative indices 39
- H True, iffy, false
  (whether, and in what circumstances, a given
  statement about powers is true)

11 Surveys and experiments 40

A The data handling cycle

B Surveys 40

C Experiments 40

12 Speed, distance and time 41

A Calculating speed 41

B Distance–time graphs 41

C Calculating distance and time

D Mixing units 43

E Time on a calculator 44

13 Volume, surface area and density 45

A Volume of a cuboid 45

B Volume of a prism 45

C Volume of a cylinder 46

D Surface area 47

E Density 47

F Units of volume and liquid measure 48

14 Cumulative frequency 49

A How long can you hold your breath?
(data collection activity)

B Cumulative frequency tables 49

C Cumulative frequency graphs 50

D Median, quartiles and interquartile range 51

E Box-and-whisker plots 52

Mixed practice 2 53

15 Working with expressions 55

A Collecting like terms level 6 55

B Multiplying and dividing expressions

C Factorising expressions 55

D Dealing with more than one letter 56

E Expanding and factorising expressions 57

F Finding and simplifying formulas 58

16 Coordinates in three dimensions 59

A Identifying points 59

17 Cubic graphs and equations 60

A Cubic functions

B Trial and improvement 60

18 Gradients and rates 61

A Gradient of a sloping line 61

B Positive and negative gradients 61

C Interpreting a gradient as a rate 62

D Calculating with rates 63

19 Changing the subject 64

A Simple linear formulas

B Adding and subtracting algebraic expressions 64

C Formulas connecting more than two letters 65

D Squares and square roots 66

20 Probability 67

A Relative frequency 67

B Equally likely outcomes 68

C Listing outcomes 69

D Showing outcomes on a grid 70

Mixed practice 3 71

21 Large and small numbers 73

A Powers of ten 73

B Writing large numbers in different ways 73

C Standard form for large numbers 74

D Using a calculator for large numbers in standard form 74

E Standard form for small numbers 75

F Using a calculator for small numbers in standard form 75

G Standard form without a calculator 76

22 The tangent function 77

A Finding an opposite side 77

B Finding an adjacent side 77

C Finding an angle 78

D Mixed questions 78

continues >

23 Linear equations 2 80

  A Review: forming and solving equations

  B Forming equations to solve word problems 80

  C Mixed questions 81

24 Loci and constructions 82

  A The locus of points a fixed distance from a point or line 82

  B The locus of points equidistant from two points

  C The shortest route from a point to a line 82

  D The locus of points equidistant from two lines 84

  E The perpendicular from a point on a line 84

25 Equations of linear graphs 85

  A Gradient and intercept of a linear graph

  B Finding the equation of a graph 85

  C Equation of a line through two given points 86

  D Fractional gradient 87

  E Rearranging the equation of a graph 87

  F Perpendicular lines 88

  G Line of best fit 89

Mixed practice 4 90

26 Quadratic expressions and equations 93

  A Multiplying out expressions such as $(x + 1)(x + 3)$

  B Opposite corners investigation

  C Multiplying out expressions such as $(x + 1)(x - 3)$ and $(x - 1)(x - 3)$ 93

  D Factorising quadratic expressions 93

  E Solving quadratic equations 94

  F Graphs and the solutions of quadratic equations 95

  G Solving problems 96

27 Handling secondary data 97

  A Drawing conclusions from data 97

  B Percentages from a two-way table

  C Reading the fine print

  D Interpreting a large table

  E Using more than one table 98

  F Taking A-level mathematics – girls and boys (analysing a data set)

28 Solving inequalities 100

  A Review: writing and interpreting inequalities 100

  B Manipulating inequalities

  C Solving simple inequalities 100

  D Unknown on both sides

  E Multiplying or dividing by a negative number 101

  F Combined inequalities 102

29 Simultaneous equations 103

  A Puzzles involving two statements (simultaneous equations solved informally)

  B Solving equations 1 103 (subtracting one equation from another)

  C Forming and solving equations 103

  D Solving equations 2 (at least one equation involving subtraction)

  E Substitution 104

  F Graphs and simultaneous equations 105

  G Mixed questions 106

30 Sine and cosine 107

  A Finding the adjacent or opposite side from the hypotenuse and angle 107

  B Finding the hypotenuse from another side and an angle 107

  C Finding an angle 108

  D Mixed questions, including tangent and Pythagoras 108

Mixed practice 5 110

1 Triangles and polygons

A Special triangles and quadrilaterals

level 6

1 (a) Draw sketches to show how an equilateral triangle can be split into

    (i)   two right-angled triangles

    (ii) a trapezium and an equilateral triangle

    (iii) a kite and two right-angled triangles

    (iv) three isosceles triangles

    (v) a parallelogram and two different-sized equilateral triangles

    (vi) three kites

(b) Describe the symmetry of each of these ways of splitting an equilateral triangle.

B Angles of a triangle

level 6

1 (a) What special kind of triangle is triangle PQR?

(b) What special kind of triangle is triangle QRS?

(c) Find each angle marked with a small letter.

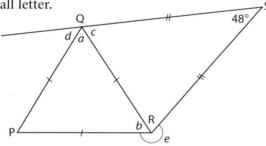

2 Calculate the angle marked **?**.

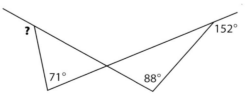

3 Find the values of x and y.

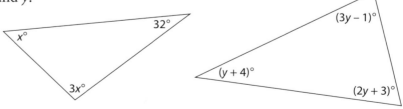

1 Find the angles marked with small letters.

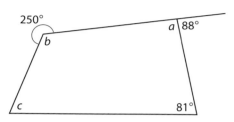

2 Find the missing angle in each of these polygons

(a)

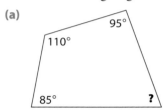

(b)

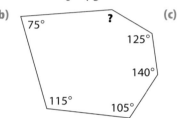

(c)

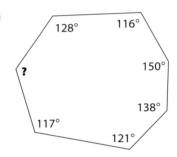

3 This is part of a regular polygon.
Point P is the centre of the polygon.

  (a) How many sides does the whole polygon have?

  (b) Find angles a, b and c.

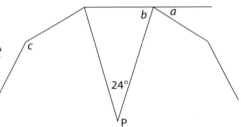

4 The sum of the interior angles of certain non-regular polygon is 1080°.
How many sides does it have?

D Mixed questions

1 This pattern is made from six regular pentagons,
all the same size.

  (a) What special type of quadrilateral is
the shaded shape in the middle?

  (b) Calculate the four angles of the
shaded quadrilateral.

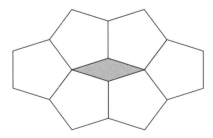

*2 What regular polygon has interior angles that are $3\frac{1}{2}$ times the size
of the exterior angles?

2 Drawing and using quadratic graphs

You need graph paper for sections A and B.

A Parabolas and quadratic functions

1 (a) Copy and complete this table of values for the equation $y = 3x^2 - 4$.

x	$^-3$	$^-2$	$^-1$	0	1	2	3
x^2	9	4			1		9
$3x^2$	27	12			3		
$y = 3x^2 - 4$	23	8			$^-1$		

(b) On graph paper, draw the graph of $y = 3x^2 - 4$ for values of x from $^-3$ to 3.

(c) Use your graph to solve the equation $3x^2 - 4 = 15$, correct to 1 d.p.

(d) What is the minimum value of y?

2 (a) Copy and complete this table of values for the equation $y = x^2 + 2x$.

x	$^-3$	$^-2$	$^-1$	0	1	2	3
x^2	9				1		
$2x$	$^-6$				2		
$y = x^2 + 2x$	3				3		

(b) On graph paper, draw the graph of $y = x^2 + 2x$ for values of x from $^-3$ to 3.

(c) Use your graph to solve the equation $x^2 + 2x = 2$, correct to 1 d.p.

(d) What is the minimum value of $x^2 + 2x$?

3 (a) Copy and complete this table of values for the equation $y = 8 - x^2$.

x	$^-3$	$^-2$	$^-1$	0	1	2	3
x^2	9	4					
$y = 8 - x^2$	$^-1$						

(b) On graph paper, draw the graph of $y = 8 - x^2$ for values of x from $^-3$ to 3.

(c) Explain why there is no solution to the equation $8 - x^2 = 9$.

(d) (i) Write down the maximum value of $8 - x^2$.

(ii) What value of x gives this maximum value?

(e) (i) Use your graph to solve the equation $8 - x^2 = 0$, correct to 1 d.p.

(ii) Hence estimate the value of the positive square root of 8.

4 (a) Copy and complete this table of values for the equation $y = x^2 - 3x - 1$.

x	-3	-2	-1	0	1	2	3	4	5
y	17								

(b) On graph paper, draw the graph of $y = x^2 - 3x - 1$ for values of x from ⁻3 to 5.

(c) Use your graph to solve $x^2 - 3x - 1 = 0$, correct to 1 d.p.

(d) On your graph draw the line of symmetry of $y = x^2 - 3x - 1$.
Write down the equation of the line of symmetry.

(e) (i) What value of x makes y a minimum?

(ii) Substitute this value into the equation and so calculate the minimum value of y.

(iii) Compare this value with the minimum value given by your graph.
How accurate was your graph?

5 (a) Copy and complete this table of values for $y = 2x^2 - 4x + 1$.

x	-2	-1	0	1	2	3	4
y	17						

(b) On graph paper, draw the graph of $y = 2x^2 - 4x + 1$ for values of x from ⁻2 to 4.

(c) Write down the equation of the line of symmetry.

(d) What is the minimum value of $2x^2 - 4x + 1$?

(e) Solve the equation $2x^2 - 4x + 1 = 2$, correct to 1 d.p.

6 (a) Copy and complete this table of values for $y = 3 + x - x^2$.

x	-3	-2	-1	0	1	2	3	4
y	-9							

(b) On graph paper, draw the graph of $y = 3 + x - x^2$ for values of x from ⁻3 to 4.

(c) Write down the equation of the line of symmetry.

(d) Calculate the maximum value of $3 + x - x^2$.

(e) Solve the equation $3 + x - x^2 = 0$, correct to 1 d.p.

(f) Show that there is no solution to the equation $3 + x - x^2 = 6$.

B Using graphs to solve problems

1

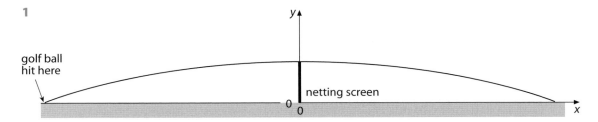

golf ball hit here

netting screen

The diagram shows the path of a golf ball.

The equation of the path of the ball is $y = 9 - \dfrac{x^2}{3600}$ (x and y are measured in metres).

(a) (i) Find the value of y when $x = 0$.

   (ii) The golf ball just clears the netting screen shown.
         How high is the screen?

(b) (i) Find the value of y when $x = 180$.

   (ii) What horizontal distance does the ball travel when it is in the air?

2 In a game a marble is pushed off the edge of a box.

The equation of the path of the marble is $y = 75 - \dfrac{x^2}{50}$
(x and y are measured in cm).

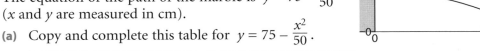

(a) Copy and complete this table for $y = 75 - \dfrac{x^2}{50}$.

x	0	10	20	30	40	50	60	70
y		73			43			

(b) On graph paper, draw the graph of $y = 75 - \dfrac{x^2}{50}$ for x from 0 to 70.

(c) How far from the bottom of the box does the marble land?

3 A stone is dropped from a tower.
The height of the stone above the ground is given by $h = 45 - 5t^2$.
h is the height of the stone in metres.
t is the time in seconds from the release of the stone.

(a) Work out the values of h for $t = 0, 0.5, 1, 1.5, \ldots$ up to $t = 3$.

(b) Draw the graph of $h = 45 - 5t^2$ for these values of t.

(c) (i) Use your graph to solve the equation $45 - 5t^2 = 22.5$.

   (ii) What is the meaning of your answer?

(d) Keeley says, 'From the graph I conclude that the stone landed 3 metres
     away from the bottom of the tower.'
     Comment on what Keeley said.

3 Distributions and averages

You need squared paper for sections BC and E.

| A Review: mean, median, range and mode | level 6 |

1 Some classes do a memory experiment with ten objects.
They look at a tray of objects and then try to remember as many as possible.

(a) Here are the results for class 10Y.

> 4 8 7 7 5 7 8 7 7 10 7 7 8 6 7 6 7 7 8 9

These numbers show how many objects each student remembered.

    (i)   What is the mean number of objects remembered for 10Y?

    (ii) What is the median number of objects remembered?

    (iii) Find the modal number of objects remembered.

    (iv) Work out the range.

(b) The results for class 10T are these.

> 8 7 7 9 9 6 8 7 9 7 8 9 8 7 4 7 8 8 9 7 10 7 8 9 9

Find the mean, median, mode and range for this data.

(c) Which class do you think did better at remembering the objects?
Give a reason for your answer.

2 An angling club recorded the weights of trout caught one day.

> **Weights of trout (in ounces)**
> 15, 31, 8, 12, 25, 19, 9, 21, 29, 21,
> 17, 23, 13, 19, 21, 26, 11, 24, 18

(a) Put this data into a stem-and-leaf table.

(b) Use your table to find the median weight of the fish.

(c) Write down the range of the weights.

(d) This is the data for trout caught on a second stretch of the river.
Use this table to find the median weight of the trout
caught on the second stretch of the river.

(e) Compare the weights of trout caught in the
two stretches of river.

0	7
1	1 1 4 6 7 8 8 9
2	2 3 4 5 6 6 9 9 9
3	0 1 3 5 8
4	1

stem = 10 ounces

3 Here are the test results for class 10M arranged in a stem-and-leaf table.

Find

(a) the median mark

(b) the range of marks

(c) the modal mark

Marks out of 20

```
0 | 8 8 9 9 9 9
1 | 0 1 1 2 5 5 6 7 8 8 9 9 9
2 | 0 0 0 0 0 0
```

4 This double stem-and-leaf table shows the speeds in m.p.h. of vehicles on a straight and a winding stretch of road.

Write a couple of sentences comparing the two sets of data.

Straight		Winding
8	2	1 3 3 4 5 6 8
8 5 5 3	3	4 5 5 6 7 7 8
8 7 6 6 4	4	0 1
9 5 2	5	
7 3	6	

stem = 10 m.p.h.

5 The number of people in cars that passed a set of traffic lights was recorded. The data recorded is shown in the table below.

Number of people in car	Number of cars
1	10
2	15
3	12
4	6
5	7
6	5

(a) How many cars were surveyed?

(b) How many people were there altogether in the cars?

(c) Calculate the mean number of people per car.

6 The weight of eggs laid by a hen over a period of four weeks is shown in the table. Calculate the mean weight of the eggs.

Weight	58 g	59 g	60 g	61 g	62 g	63 g
Number of eggs	3	7	11	9	8	2

7 A group of students does a memory experiment with fifteen words.

Their results are shown in this table.

Find the mean, median, mode and range for this data.

Number of words remembered	Number of people
5	2
6	3
7	4
8	8
9	15
10	7
11	6
12	1

1 This data gives the length in centimetres (*l*) from nose to tail of some grey squirrels.

44.9	42.0	48.9	35.2	49.0	45.5	51.6	47.1	49.4	44.2	51.2	45.4	49.0
54.5	39.5	41.3	41.3	58.7	49.8	32.7	41.2	45.3	39.0	54.7	49.5	42.3
46.4	51.7	49.3	38.7									

(a) Copy and complete this frequency table for the lengths of squirrels.

Length (*l* cm)	Tally	Frequency
$30.0 \leq l < 35.0$		
$35.0 \leq l < 40.0$		
$40.0 \leq l < 45.0$		

(b) Draw a frequency diagram of this data on squared paper.

(c) What is the modal group for this data?

2 The data below shows the weights (*w*) of some students in kilograms.

65	63	50	52	42	68	72	67	46	54	43	64	51	46	57	43	45	62	54	49
48	55	64	60	50	66	55	51	49	43	73	56	58	47	61	58	59	57	56	51

(a) Put this data into a grouped frequency table with intervals
     $40 \leq w < 50$, $50 \leq w < 60$, $60 \leq w < 70$, …
     Find the modal group of the weights.

(b) Put this data into a grouped frequency table with intervals
     $40 \leq w < 45$, $45 \leq w < 50$, $50 \leq w < 55$, …
     Find the modal group of the weights.

(c) Which of the two sets of intervals gives a clearer picture of
     the distribution of the weights?

3 The lengths of 36 runner beans were measured and rounded to the nearest mm.

152	180	165	182	177	160	172	183	163	185	159	176
186	173	189	191	176	192	178	175	173	186	188	193
162	189	168	184	153	170	155	166	184	179	174	171

(a) Make a frequency table for the given data.
     Choose your own class intervals

(b) Draw a frequency chart for the data.

D Estimating a mean using mid-interval values

1 A disc jockey was planning a radio show.

This table shows the length of record to be played and some unfinished working to estimate the mean length of the records.

Time (t min)	Frequency	Mid-interval value	Group total estimate
$1 \leq t < 2$	1	1.5	$1 \times 1.5 = 1.5$
$2 \leq t < 3$	3	2.5	$3 \times 2.5 = 7.5$
$3 \leq t < 4$	27	3.5	$27 \times 3.5 =$
$4 \leq t < 5$	32		
$5 \leq t < 6$	8		
Total	71		

(a) How many records lasted three minutes or more?

(b) Copy and complete the table above.

(c) Use your table to estimate

    (i) the total length of the show   **(ii)** the mean length of the records

2 This bar chart gives information about the weight of a sample of 100 eggs.

(a) Use the chart to write out a grouped frequency table with groups $60 \leq w < 65$, $65 \leq w < 70$, … and so on.

(b) Use your table to find an estimate of the mean weight of the eggs.

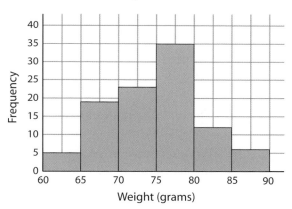

3 The data below shows the amount of rain in millimetres that fell each day in February.

```
3.5  16.4  6.4  3.7  14.2  8.9  22.9  2.9  7.8  13.9
14.2  4.5  11.6  15.9  18.9  0.1  6.1  1.4  3.1
2.5  5.6  2.6  9.4  4.1  17.9  19.2  10.7  7.2
```

(a) Draw a frequency table to show this information.
You will need to choose sensible groups for the data.

(b) Calculate an estimate for the mean daily rainfall in February.

(c) Calculate the mean of the actual daily rainfall and compare the two results.

4 For her geography project Nina collects data about the weekly rainfall (*d*) in millimetres for her home town. She displays the results in a table.

Calculate an estimate for the mean weekly rainfall.

Weekly rainfall (*d*) in mm	Number of weeks
$0 < d \leq 10$	18
$10 < d \leq 20$	20
$20 < d \leq 30$	3
$30 < d \leq 40$	4
$40 < d \leq 50$	3
$50 < d \leq 60$	4

E Frequency polygons

1 This table shows the age distribution of the people living in a village.

Draw a frequency polygon for the data.

Age (*A* years)	Frequency
$0 < A \leq 20$	12
$20 < A \leq 40$	28
$40 < A \leq 60$	34
$60 < A \leq 80$	11
$80 < A \leq 100$	3

2 The armspans of students in classes 10M and 9P are measured. The results are displayed in this table.

(a) On the same axes draw frequency polygons for the armspans for 10M and 9P.

(b) Calculate estimates for the mean armspan for each class.

(c) Write a couple of sentences comparing the armspans of 10M and 9P.

Armspan (*a* cm)	Frequency 10M	Frequency 9P
$150 < a \leq 155$	3	4
$155 < a \leq 160$	5	7
$160 < a \leq 165$	7	10
$165 < a \leq 170$	8	6
$170 < a \leq 175$	6	3
$175 < a \leq 180$	1	0

3 A group of children and a group of adults take part in an experiment in which each person is timed carrying out an unfamiliar task.

The frequency polygons show the distributions of the times taken by each group.

(a) By looking at the diagram, decide which group had the longer mean time.

(b) How many people were in each group?

(c) Calculate an estimate of the mean time for each group.

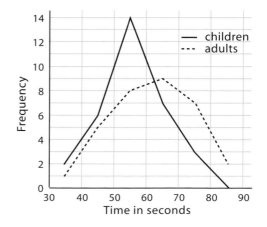

4 Fractions

B Reciprocals

1 Write down the reciprocal of each of these.

(a) 7   (b) $\frac{8}{15}$ (c) $\frac{1}{9}$ (d) $1\frac{1}{4}$ (e) $3\frac{1}{2}$

2 Find the reciprocal of each of these.

(a) 0.2   (b) 0.8   (c) 0.04   (d) 1.6   (e) 12.5

C Dividing by a fraction

1 Work these out.

(a) $12 \div \frac{1}{3}$ (b) $6 \div \frac{2}{3}$ (c) $8 \div \frac{2}{5}$ (d) $2 \div \frac{3}{5}$ (e) $5 \div \frac{3}{4}$

2 Work these out.

(a) $\frac{2}{7} \div \frac{1}{3}$ (b) $\frac{3}{5} \div \frac{2}{3}$ (c) $\frac{3}{4} \div \frac{5}{8}$ (d) $1\frac{1}{2} \div \frac{1}{4}$ (e) $2\frac{1}{4} \div 1\frac{1}{2}$

D Mixed questions

1 Work these out.

(a) $\frac{7}{8} - \frac{2}{5}$ (b) $\frac{9}{10} + \frac{1}{3}$ (c) $\frac{2}{3} \times \frac{5}{8}$ (d) $\frac{3}{10} \div 2$ (e) $1\frac{2}{3} + \frac{3}{5}$

(f) $4\frac{1}{3} - 2\frac{9}{10}$ (g) $\frac{3}{5}$ of $\frac{11}{12}$ (h) $8 \times \frac{7}{12}$ (i) $\frac{2}{3} \div \frac{7}{8}$ (j) $1\frac{1}{4} \times 2\frac{2}{3}$

2 At a dog kennels, 12 tins of dog food are shared out so that each dog gets $\frac{3}{4}$ of a tin. How many dogs will this feed?

3 $\frac{3}{5}$ of a number is 45. What is the number?

4 Given that $x = \frac{1}{3}$, $y = \frac{1}{4}$ and $z = \frac{2}{5}$, find the value of each of these.

(a) $y + z$ (b) $z - x$ (c) $4x - 1$ (d) $\frac{y}{z}$ (e) $xy + z$

5 Solve these equations.

(a) $\frac{1}{6}x = \frac{5}{8}$ (b) $\frac{3}{4}x = \frac{7}{8}$ (c) $\frac{2}{5}x = \frac{6}{7}$ (d) $\frac{5}{8}x = \frac{1}{3}$

6 In an election there were 4 candidates: Arjan, Bess, Colin and Diane.
Between 400 and 450 people voted.
Exactly $\frac{2}{5}$ voted for Arjan, $\frac{1}{3}$ for Bess and $\frac{1}{4}$ for Colin.

(a) How many people voted altogether?

(b) How many voted for Diane?

5 Accuracy

A Lower and upper bounds

1 Round 56 372 to the nearest

    (a) ten   (b) hundred   (c) thousand   (d) ten thousand

2 Round each of these decimals to the nearest whole number.

    (a) 65.43   (b) 1.8702   (c) 420.695   (d) 109.58

3 Write down the lower and upper bounds for the length in each sentence.

    (a) The length of a pencil is 64 mm to the nearest whole millimetre.

    (b) The radius of a wheel is 50 cm to the nearest whole centimetre.

    (c) The length of a path is 250 m to the nearest ten metres.

    (d) The width of a flower bed is 410 cm to the nearest ten centimetres.

    (e) The length of a cycle route is 5400 m to the nearest hundred metres.

4 Write down the minimum and maximum possible values for each of these amounts.

    (a) The height of a boy is 144 cm, correct to the nearest centimetre.

    (b) The capacity of a jug is 350 ml, correct to the nearest 10 ml.

    (c) The weight of a parcel, to the nearest 100 g, is 1500 g.

    (d) The population of a town is 56 000, correct to the nearest thousand.

5 The temperature in an oven is measured as 220 °C to the nearest 10 degrees.
What are the lower and upper bounds for the temperature in the oven?

6 A bucket contains 4500 ml of water, correct to the nearest 100 ml.
What are the lower and upper bounds for the amount of water in the bucket?

7 The length of a worksurface is measured as 1370 mm, correct to the nearest millimetre.
What are the lower and upper bounds for this length?

8 The attendance at a football match is reported as 18 000, correct to the nearest hundred.
What are the lower and upper bounds for the attendance at the match?

*9 Jack measures a space in his kitchen as 60 cm wide, correct to the nearest centimetre.
Explain why a washing machine of width 60 cm, correct to the nearest centimetre
may not fit in this space.

*10 Sadie measures the width of her bedroom as 210 cm, correct to the nearest 10 cm.
She buys a bed measuring 208 cm, correct to the nearest centimetre.
Explain why the bed may not fit across the width of the bedroom.

6 Linear equations 1

A Solving equations

1 Solve each equation.
  Give each non-integer solution as a fraction in its simplest form.

  (a) $6p - 1 = 2$ (b) $3(n + 5) = 6n$ (c) $5x + 18 = 8 - 5x$

  (d) $3(4k + 3) = 18$ (e) $5y - 13 = 11 - 3y$ (f) $3(2d + 1) = 2d - 5$

  (g) $2(8 - 3m) = 11$ (h) $5(2 - a) = a - 8$ (i) $2(2q + 5) = q + 3$

2 Solve each equation.

  (a) $5(x - 2) = 2(x + 1)$ (b) $2(3x - 2) = 5(x + 7)$ (c) $3(4x - 5) = 10(x - 1)$

  (d) $3(4x - 1) = 2(1 + x)$ (e) $2(5x + 8) = 3(2x + 5)$ (f) $2(5x - 1) = 7(x + 4)$

  (g) $3(1 - 2x) = 5(x + 5)$ (h) $3(2x + 1) = 8(4x - 11)$ (i) $3(4 - 3x) = 9(5 - 2x)$

3 Solve each equation.

  (a) $4(n - 1) + n = 36$ (b) $4(3n - 2) - 2n = 12$

  (c) $2(3n - 1) + 4(n + 5) = 58$ (d) $3(4n + 11) - 2(3n + 2) = 17$

  (e) $4(2n + 3) - 5(3n + 2) = 9$ (f) $6(4n - 3) - 3(5 - 2n) = 57$

B Forming equations

1 Work out the starting number in each of these number puzzles.

  (a)
  | I think of a number. |
  | I multiply it by 2. |
  | I subtract 4. |
  | My answer is 11. |

  (b)
  | I think of a number. |
  | I add 10. |
  | I multiply the result by 5. |
  | The answer is 35. |

2 These two triangles have the same perimeter.

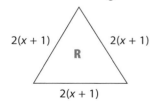
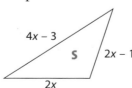

  (a) Write an expression in x for the perimeter of each triangle.

  (b) Form an equation and solve it to find the value of x.

  (c) What is the perimeter of each triangle?

3 Solve each of these number puzzles.

(a)
> I think of a number.
> I add 5.
> I multiply the result by 4.
> My answer is double the number I first thought of.
> What was my number?

(b)
> I think of a number.
> I add 1 to it.
> I multiply the result by 3.
> My answer is 21 more than the number I started with.
> What was my number?

4 Find the size of each angle in these shapes.

(a)

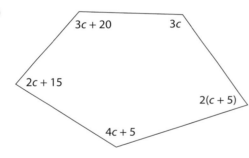

(b)

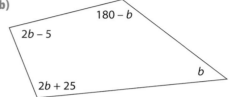

(c)

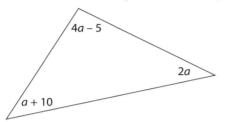

(d)

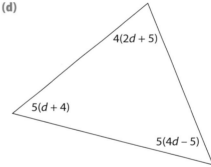

5 Work out the starting number in each of these 'think of a number' puzzles.

(a) Jack and Alex both think of the same number.

Jack subtracts 8 and then multiplies the result by 6.
Alex doubles the number and then subtracts 8.

They both end up with the same number.

(b) Narinder and Brian both think of the same number.

Narinder adds 5 to her number and multiplies the result by 3.
Brian adds 3 to the number and then multiplies by 9.

They both end up with the same number.

c Equations that involve a fraction
d More than one fraction

1 Solve these equations.

(a) $\dfrac{x}{3} = 9$

(b) $\dfrac{1}{2}x + 5 = 2$

(c) $\dfrac{x-2}{7} = 2$

(d) $\dfrac{1+5x}{2} = 4$

(e) $\dfrac{4x+11}{3} = 3$

(f) $\dfrac{3-x}{8} = 1$

2 Solve these equations.

(a) $\dfrac{8+x}{5} = x$

(b) $\dfrac{2x-20}{7} = x$

(c) $\dfrac{20-4x}{3} = 2x$

(d) $\dfrac{3x+1}{2} = 2x + 3$

(e) $\dfrac{5x-2}{3} = 3x - 10$

(f) $\dfrac{1+2x}{4} = 4 - x$

3 Work out the starting number in each of these 'think of a number' puzzles.

(a)
I think of a number.
I divide by 5.
I then add 1.
My answer is 4.

(b)
I think of a number.
I add 8.
I then divide by 3.
My answer is 2.

(c)
I think of a number.
I add 22.
I then divide by 6.
My answer is double the number I first thought of.

4 Solve these equations.

(a) $\dfrac{x-2}{2} = \dfrac{x+4}{3}$

(b) $\dfrac{x-1}{5} = \dfrac{x-7}{2}$

(c) $\dfrac{3x+3}{4} = \dfrac{5x-6}{3}$

(d) $\dfrac{4x+1}{5} = \dfrac{5x+2}{6}$

(e) $\dfrac{6x-2}{3} = \dfrac{2(4x+1)}{5}$

(f) $\dfrac{1}{2}(6x-3) = \dfrac{1}{5}(8x+3)$

5 Solve these equations.

(a) $\dfrac{x+5}{2} + \dfrac{2x-9}{5} = 7$

(b) $\dfrac{3x-5}{4} + \dfrac{3-x}{2} = x$

(c) $\dfrac{5x-3}{4} - \dfrac{2x+1}{5} = 5$

(d) $\dfrac{6x+1}{2} - \dfrac{4x+1}{3} = 2x$

6 Solve these equations.

(a) $\dfrac{3}{4}x + 1 = 16$

(b) $8 - \dfrac{x}{5} = 2(x-7)$

(c) $\dfrac{1}{5}(2x+3) + \dfrac{2}{3}(3-x) = 1$

7 The mean of the three numbers $(x-3)$, $(x+2)$ and $(2x-11)$ is 10.
Form an equation and solve it to find the value of x.

*8 A number is added to the numerator of the fraction $\frac{3}{5}$.
The resulting expression is equivalent to $\frac{2}{3}$.
What number was added to the numerator?

7 Area and perimeter

A Parallelogram level 6

1 Find the areas of these parallelograms.

(a)

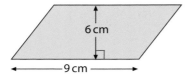

6 cm

9 cm

(b)

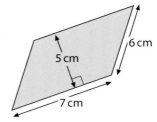

6 cm

5 cm

7 cm

2 (a) Calculate the area of each parallelogram, to 1 d.p.

(b) Find the perimeter of each parallelogram.

(i)

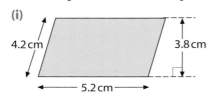

4.2 cm

3.8 cm

5.2 cm

(ii)

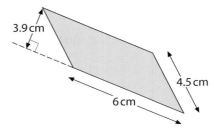

3.9 cm

6 cm

4.5 cm

3 These are two parallelograms.
Find the lengths marked by letters.

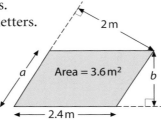

2 m

a

Area = 3.6 m²

b

2.4 m

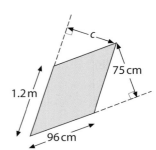

c

75 cm

1.2 m

96 cm

B Triangle level 6

1 Find the areas of these triangles, rounding to one decimal place where you need to.

(a)

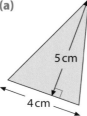

5 cm

4 cm

(b)

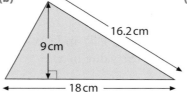

16.2 cm

9 cm

18 cm

(c)

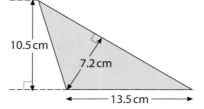

10.5 cm

7.2 cm

13.5 cm

2 These two triangles have the same area.
Find the lengths marked by letters.

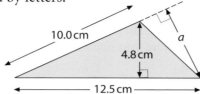 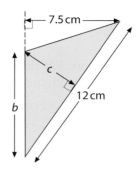

C Composite shapes and algebra

1 Calculate the area of each of these shapes,
rounding to one decimal place where you need to.

(a)

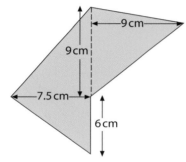

(b)

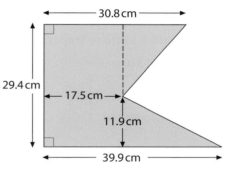

2 Write down expressions for the areas of the shaded triangles.
Simplify your answers as far as possible.

(a)

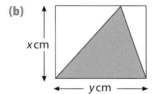

(b)

(c)

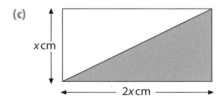

3 (a) Write, as simply as possible, an
expression for the area of each shape.

(b) Find the value of *a* that gives both
shapes the same area.

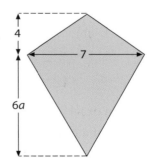 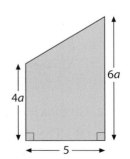

D Trapezium

1 Work out the area of each of these shapes.
   Round to one decimal place where you need to.

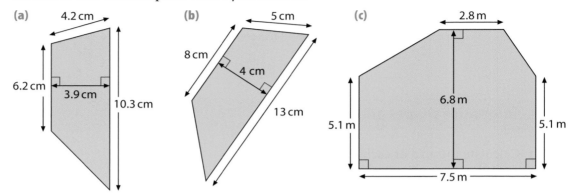

(a) 4.2 cm, 6.2 cm, 3.9 cm, 10.3 cm

(b) 5 cm, 8 cm, 4 cm, 13 cm

(c) 2.8 m, 6.8 m, 5.1 m, 5.1 m, 7.5 m

2 Find a and b in these trapeziums.

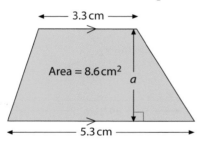

Area = 8.6 cm^2, 3.3 cm, a, 5.3 cm

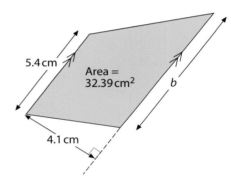

5.4 cm, Area = 32.39 cm^2, b, 4.1 cm

E Circle

1 Using the π key on your calculator find **(i)** the circumference and **(ii)** the area
   of each of these circles. (Give your answers to 1 d.p.)

(a) 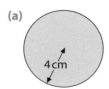 4 cm

(b) 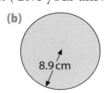 8.9 cm

(c) 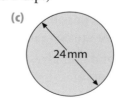 24 mm

(d) 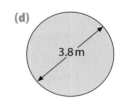 3.8 m

2 Give each of these as an exact value containing π.

   (a) The circumference of a circle with radius 6 units

   (b) The area of a circle with radius 4 units

   (c) The area of a circle with diameter 10 units

   (d) The perimeter of a semicircle with diameter 14 units

Give your answers for the rest of this section to one decimal place.

3 Find the radius of a circle that has a circumference of (a) 48 cm   (b) 24 cm

4 The circumference of a car tyre is 186 cm.
What is the diameter of the tyre?

5 A piece of string 80 cm long is made into a loop.
   (a) What is the diameter of the largest circle that can
        be surrounded by the string?
   (b) What is the area of this circle?

6 Find the radius of a circle that has an area of   (a) 36 cm²   (b) 54 cm²

7 On a ride, the front wheel of a penny-farthing bicycle turned 125 times.
The bike travelled 589 m.
   (a) Find the diameter of the front wheel.
   (b) The rear wheel turned 490 times on the ride.
        What is the ratio of the diameter of the
        front wheel to the diameter of the rear wheel?

F Population density

1 (a) France has an area of 551 695 km² and its population is 61 538 000.
        Calculate the population density of France.
   (b) The area of Germany is 357 021 km² and the population density is 231 per km².
        Calculate an approximate figure for the population of Germany.

2 This table shows typical yields from some vegetables.
   (a) What weight of potatoes should you get from
        a plot with area 20.5 m²?
   (b) What weight of broad beans should you get from
        a rectangular plot 4.2 m by 1.5 m?
   (c) How many cucumbers should you get from a
        rectangular plot 2.5 m by 0.5 m?

Vegetable	Yield
Aubergine	5.0 kg/m²
Broad bean	3.8 kg/m²
French bean	2.5 kg/m²
Cucumber	16 cucumbers/m²
Potato	4.0 kg/m²

   (d) What area is needed to get 22 kg of broad beans (to the nearest 0.1 m²)?
   (e) A gardener has a plot with area 6.5 m².
        He wants to fill it, growing aubergines and French beans only.
        He wants the weight of French beans he grows to be twice the weight of aubergines.
        What area should he give to each crop and what weights would he expect to get?

G Converting units of area

1 A rectangular tablecloth measures 150 cm by 240 cm.
   (a) Calculate the area of the cloth in cm².   **(b)** Convert your answer to m².

2 A piece of paper measures 0.6 m by 0.45 m.
   (a) Calculate the area of the paper in m².   **(b)** Convert your answer to cm².

3 A credit card measures 8.5 cm by 5.4 cm.
   (a) Calculate the area of the card in cm².   **(b)** Convert your answer to mm².

4 A farm has an area of 450 hectares.
   What area is this in   **(a)** m²   **(b)** km²

5 The surface area of a box is 5250 mm². What is this area in cm²?

H Mixed questions

1 A shape consists of a square of side 5 cm and
   a semicircle as shown.

   Calculate the area of the shape,

   (a) in cm²

   (b) in mm²

2 Calculate each of the blue areas.

   (a)
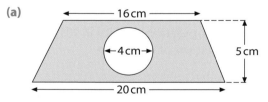

   (b)
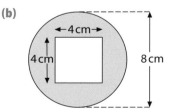

3 The pattern contains five circles.
   Two of the white circles have a radius of 4 units and
   the other two white circles have a radius of 6 units.

   Find each of the following as an exact value.

   (a) the area of circle A

   (b) the area of circle B

   (c) the area of the large circle

   (d) the area shaded black

   (e) the ratio of black area to white area in its simplest form

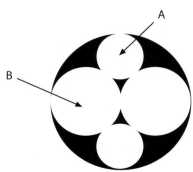

8 Percentages

A Review: percentage change

1 Write down the decimal equivalent of

   (a) 46%   (b) 8%   (c) 35.2%   (d) 112%   (e) 7.5%

2 (a) Increase £125 by 18%.   (b) Decrease £150 by 22%.

3 A shop reduces prices by 12% in a sale.
   What is the sale price of a coat costing £135?

4 A firm is going to give its workers a 5% pay rise.
   What will be the new rate of pay of a worker earning £8.60 per hour?

5 A car costing £15 000 when new was sold for £11 400 when it was one year old.
   What was the percentage decrease in value?

6 A 330 ml can of drink costs 52p.
   The can is to be replaced by a 500 ml can costing 69p. Calculate

   (a) the percentage increase in the size

   (b) the percentage increase in the cost

   (c) the percentage change in the cost per litre

B Successive percentage changes

1 Calculate the overall percentage change for each of these.

   (a) A 15% increase then a 10% increase

   (b) An 8% decrease then a 12.5% decrease

   (c) A 12% increase then a 12% decrease

   (d) A 10% decrease then a 20% increase then a 15% decrease

   (e) A 16.8% increase then a 8.2% decrease then a 12.6% decrease

2 The population of gulls nesting on an island is expected to decrease by 8%
   during next year and then by 8% during the year after that.
   The population now is 17 400.
   What is it expected to be in two years' time, to the nearest hundred?

3 Joe's garage put up the prices of all its cars by 4% in January.
   In March, prices were reduced by 10%.
   What was the final price, to the nearest £10, of a car that cost £3470 before January?

4 Over the past three years, the volume of water in a pond has decreased by 10% each year. What is the overall percentage decrease over the three years?

5 Last year a travel agent increased the price of a holiday to Spain by 8%. This year the price was decreased by 5%. What was the overall percentage increase in price?

*6 Over two years the average attendance at a football ground increased by 26%. The attendance increased by 15% in the first year. What was the percentage increase during the second year?

c Compound interest

1 £650 is put into a bank account which pays interest at the rate of 6% per annum.

Copy and complete this table showing the amount in the account at the end of each year.
(Round your answers to the nearest penny.)

Years	Amount
0	£650.00
1	£689.00
2	
3	
4	

2 Calculate the final amount when £850 is invested at 3.75% p.a. for 12 years.

3 Which of these gives the larger amount? Show your working.

   Investing £500 for 3 years at 4% p.a. **or** Investing £500 for 4 years at 3% p.a.

4 £2000 is invested in an account which pays interest at 6% per annum. How many years will it have to stay in the account before it is worth £3000?

5 The number of people attending a cinema decreased by 6% every year. What was the overall percentage decrease in attendances over 3 years?

6 A bank charges interest on a loan at a rate of 1.8% per month. Calculate, to the nearest 0.1%, the overall percentage rate per year.

D Percentage change in reverse

1 The population of a town has increased by 5% during the last ten years. The present population is 16 000. What was the population ten years ago? (Round your answer to the nearest 100.)

2 A television costs £399. This price includes VAT at 17.5%. What is the cost of the television before VAT is added?

3 A shop reduced the price of shoes by 25% in a sale.
   A pair of shoes cost £24 in the sale.
   What was the price of the pair of shoes before it was reduced for the sale?

4 A restaurant adds a service charge of 12% to each bill.
   A customer in the restaurant paid £19.60, including the service charge, for a meal.
   What was the price of the meal before the service charge was added?

5 The cost of a drawing program was reduced by 10% to £89.99.
   What was the cost of the software before the reduction?

6 The number of viewers watching a weekly television programme increased
   by 15% when an episode showed the two stars getting married.
   5.4 million watched the wedding episode.

   How many more people watched the wedding episode than the episode
   the previous week? (Give your answer correct to one significant figure.)

7 A magazine's sales figures have dropped by 12% in the past year to 32 478.
   How many more copies did the magazine sell last year?

E Mixed questions

1 Given that the rate of VAT is 17.5%, calculate
   (a) the price including VAT of a scanner advertised as '£66 plus VAT'
   (b) the price excluding VAT of a printer advertised as '£150.40 including VAT'

2 The population of squirrels in a wood has increased from 1250 to 1350 in the past year.
   (a) What was the percentage increase in the population during the past year?
   (b) If there is the same percentage increase in the next year, what will the
        population be in one year's time?
   (c) If the population always goes up by the same percentage in a year, what was
        the population one year before it was 1250 (to the nearest whole number)?

3 A garage owner reduced the selling price of a car from £6299 to £5999.
   (a) What was the percentage reduction in price?
   (b) He still could not sell the car so he reduced its price by a further 7.5%.
        What was the final selling price (to the nearest £)?
   (c) Calculate the overall percentage decrease in price.

4 The owner of a toll bridge increased the toll for cars crossing the bridge by 8%.
   As a consequence, 5% of the drivers who used the bridge decided
   to use an alternative route.
   Calculate the percentage change in toll money taken.

Mixed practice 1

You need graph paper.

1 The expressions in the triangle give the size of each angle in degrees.

    (a) Find the value of n.

    (b) Show that the triangle is isosceles.

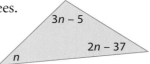

2 A firm making matches checked the contents of 120 boxes. The data is in this table.

Number of matches in box	46	47	48	49	50	51
Number of boxes	10	22	48	19	15	6

    (a) Find the range.

    (b) Calculate the mean number of matches in a box, correct to 1 d.p.

3 Hal invested £4000 at a rate of 3% per annum compound interest. How much will the investment be worth at the end of four years?

4 Find the reciprocal of $2\frac{1}{3}$.

5 Carla fires a plastic 'rocket' straight up in the air from a toy launcher. The rocket's height, h metres, is given by the formula

$$h = 24t - 5t^2$$

where t is the time in seconds from when Carla fires the rocket.

    (a) Copy and complete this table.

t	0	1	2	3	4	5	6
$h = 24t - 5t^2$	0	19					

    (b) Using suitable axes on graph paper, draw the graph of $h = 24t - 5t^2$.

    (c) **(i)** From the graph, what is the greatest height reached by the rocket?

        (ii) At what value of t does it reach this height?

    (d) When does the rocket hit the ground?

6 A bag of flour contains 1500 grams to the nearest 10 grams. What are the upper and lower bounds for the weight of the bag of flour?

7 The diagram shows part of a regular polygon. Calculate the number of sides of the polygon.

8 The diagram shows a quadrilateral.

    (a) What is the name of this quadrilateral?

    (b) The perimeter of the shape is 32 cm. Find the area of the shape.

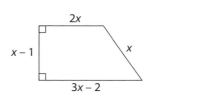

9 A circular frame for a mirror is made up of eight pieces, each like this.

14.5 cm

To the nearest 0.1 cm, calculate the radius of the mirror that fits in the frame.

10 This table shows the distribution of the weights of some babies.

Weight (w kg)	Frequency
$3.0 < w \leq 3.5$	8
$3.5 < w \leq 4.0$	14
$4.0 < w \leq 4.5$	11
$4.5 < w \leq 5.0$	7

(a) What is the modal class?

(b) Draw a frequency polygon for this data.

(c) Calculate an estimate of the mean weight of the babies.

11 Solve these equations.

(a) $7x + 2 = 4x + 3$ (b) $5(3x + 1) = 2(2x - 3)$ (c) $4(2x - 1) - 3(x + 1) = 7x$

12 Work these out.

(a) $\frac{1}{4} + \frac{2}{3}$ (b) $\frac{2}{3} \times \frac{3}{4}$ (c) $2\frac{1}{2} - 1\frac{3}{5}$ (d) $1\frac{1}{2} \times 2\frac{1}{3}$

(e) $4 \div \frac{2}{3}$ (f) $1 \div \frac{3}{5}$ (g) $\frac{2}{3} \div \frac{1}{2}$ (h) $\frac{2}{5} \div \frac{3}{10}$

13 The price of a camera decreases by 17% to £145.50.
What was the price of the camera before the decrease?

14 What is the value of $p + q - r$ when $p = 1\frac{1}{6}$, $q = \frac{3}{5}$ and $r = \frac{7}{10}$?
Give your answer as a mixed number in its lowest terms.

15 Solve these equations.

(a) $\dfrac{5r - 1}{8} = 3$ (b) $\dfrac{x + 7}{3} = x + 5$ (c) $\dfrac{x + 4}{4} = \dfrac{10 - x}{3}$

(d) $\dfrac{p - 7}{3} = \dfrac{3p}{2}$ (e) $\dfrac{n + 1}{4} + \dfrac{n + 2}{3} = 1$ (f) $\dfrac{y + 2}{3} - \dfrac{y + 5}{5} = 1$

16 In this diagram PQ is a diameter of a circle. R is a point on the circumference of the circle.

(a) Calculate, to 2 s.f., the shaded area

     (i) in m^2 (ii) in cm^2

(b) What percentage of the circle is not shaded?

(c) Find the perimeter of the triangle.

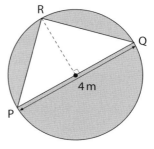

*17 A square is drawn with each vertex on the circumference of a circle.
The area of the square is 50 cm^2.
Find the exact area of the circle.

9 Transformations

You need squared paper for all sections.

A **Reflection**	level 6
B **Translation**	level 6

1 Write down the image after reflecting

  (a) shape C in line $y = 3$

  (b) shape H in line $y = {}^-x$

  (c) shape E in the y-axis

  (d) shape J in line $x = {}^-1$

2 Give the equation of the mirror line used to reflect

  (a) E on to D

  (b) C on to D

  (c) C on to A

  (d) H on to I

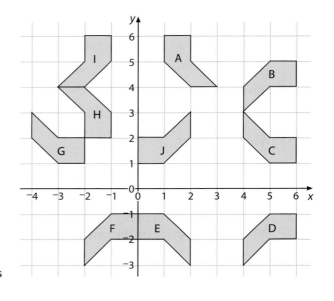

3 Describe the transformation that maps

  (a) A on to I   **(b)** B on to D

  (c) J on to C   **(d)** F on to B

4 Describe the translations needed to transform shape A on to each of the other shapes on this grid.

5 Copy the grid and shape A. Draw the image of shape A after a translation using each of these vectors.

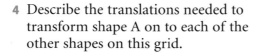

$$P \begin{bmatrix} 2 \\ -1 \end{bmatrix} \qquad Q \begin{bmatrix} 3 \\ 1 \end{bmatrix}$$

$$R \begin{bmatrix} -2 \\ -3 \end{bmatrix} \qquad S \begin{bmatrix} 0 \\ 2 \end{bmatrix}$$

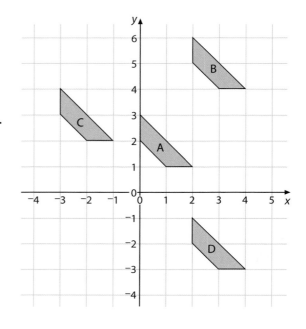

6 Draw a coordinate grid with *x*- and *y*-axes numbered from ⁻6 to 6.
On your grid draw and label shape T with vertices at (1, 3), (1, 5), (2, 5) and (3, 3).

(a) Reflect shape T in the *x*-axis. Label the image A.

(b) Reflect shape T in the line *y* = *x*. Label the image B.

(c) Reflect shape T in the line *x* = ⁻1. Label the image C.

(d) Reflect shape T in the line *y* = 2. Label the image D.

(e) What transformation would map shape A on to shape D?

c Rotation

1 Give the shape that is the image of

(a) shape A after a rotation through 180° about (3, 2)

(b) shape D after a rotation 90° anticlockwise about (0, 0)

(c) shape F after a rotation 90° clockwise about (0, ⁻1)

(d) shape H after a rotation 90° anticlockwise about (⁻2, 3)

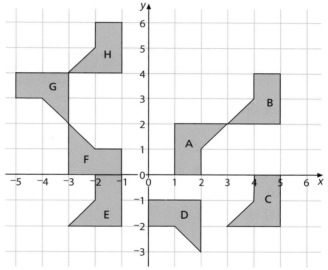

2 Describe fully the rotation that maps

(a) E on to D   (b) C on to A

(c) A on to H   (d) F on to E

3 On squared paper, draw *x*- and *y*-axes going from ⁻5 to 7.
Draw the quadrilateral with vertices at (1, 2), (1, 4), (3, 4) and (2, 2). Label it P.

(a) Draw and label the following.

Q, the image of P after a rotation 90° anticlockwise about (0, 0)
R, the image of P after a rotation through 180° about (4, 2)
S, the image of P after a rotation 90° clockwise about (4, 3)

(b) Describe fully the transformation that maps S on to R.

D Enlargement

1 On squared paper, draw *x*- and *y*-axes going from 0 to 12.
Draw the quadrilateral with vertices at (6, 4), (7, 3), (8, 4) and (8, 5). Label it D.

(a) Draw the enlargement of D with centre (5, 2) and scale factor 2.

(b) Draw the enlargement of D with centre (9, 3) and scale factor 3.

2 Copy this diagram.

(a) Describe fully the transformation that maps shape P on to shape Q.

(b) Draw an enlargement of P with scale factor $\frac{1}{2}$ and ($^-2$, $^-3$) as the centre of enlargement. Label it R.

(c) Describe fully the transformation that maps Q on to R.

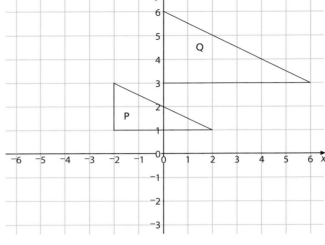

E Mixed questions

1 Describe fully the single transformation that maps

(a) A on to B

(b) C on to A

(c) A on to E

(d) C on to E

(e) C on to D

(f) E on to F

(g) F on to C

(h) B on to A

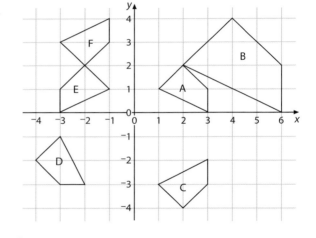

2 Draw x- and y-axes both going from $^-5$ to 5.
Draw and label triangle P with vertices (2, 1), (5, 1) and (4, 2).

(a) Rotate P 90° anticlockwise about (0, 0). Label the image Q.

(b) Reflect Q in the line $y = {^-x}$. Label the image R.

(c) What single transformation would map P directly on to R?

3 Draw axes both numbered from $^-5$ to 5.
Draw and label shape R with vertices ($^-1$, 1), ($^-1$, 3), ($^-2$, 3) and ($^-3$, 2).

(a) Rotate R 180° about (0, 2). Label the image S.

(b) Translate S by vector $\begin{bmatrix} 2 \\ -6 \end{bmatrix}$. Label the image T.

(c) What single transformation would map R directly on to T?

10 Powers and indices

A Calculating with powers

1 The diagram shows the first three patterns in a series.

Pattern 1   Pattern 2   Pattern 3

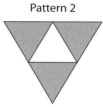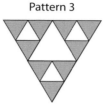

To make a new pattern, every shaded triangle is cut up into
3 shaded triangles and 1 white triangle.

How many shaded triangles will there be in

(a) pattern 4   (b) pattern 5   (c) pattern n

2 Evaluate these.
   (a) 5^0 (b) 5^3 (c) 2^1 (d) 4^2
   (e) 3^3 (f) 5^1 (g) 2^5 (h) 3^4

3 Evaluate these.
   (a) $2^5 - 8$ (b) $3^2 + 3^3$ (c) $2^3 + 7^0$ (d) $3^4 \div 3^1$
   (e) $2^2 \times 5^2$ (f) $4^3 \div 2^4$ (g) $5^3 \div 3^0$ (h) $7^1 \times 1^7$

4 Work out the value of 2×3^n when
   (a) $n = 0$ (b) $n = 1$ (c) $n = 3$ (d) $n = 4$

5 For each of the following, work out the value of p.
   (a) $2^p = 32$ (b) $5^p = 125$ (c) $p^1 = 11$ (d) $p^2 = 81$
   (e) $5^p = 1$ (f) $10^p = 1000$ (g) $2^p = 2$ (h) $p^4 = 10\,000$

6 Find the value of each of the following when $a = 2$.
   (a) $a^2 + a^3$ (b) $2a^3$ (c) $a^3 - a^2$ (d) a^5
   (e) $3a^4$ (f) $a^0 + a^1$ (g) $a^4 + a^4 + a^4$ (h) $a^2 \times a^3$

7 Work out the value of t in each of these.
   (a) $5^t + 5 = 30$ (b) $4^t \div 8 = 8$ (c) $5^2 - 4^t = 3^2$ (d) $5 \times 5^t = 625$
   (e) $10^2 \div t = 5^2$ (f) $2^t \times 5^3 = 1000$ (g) $2^5 + t^2 = 57$ (h) $t^t = 27$

B Multiplying powers
C Multiplying expressions with powers

1 Write the answers to these using indices.

(a) $5^3 \times 5^4$ (b) $7^3 \times 7^8$ (c) $5^2 \times 5^9$ (d) $9^4 \times 9^5$

(e) $2^3 \times 2^5 \times 2^7$ (f) $4 \times 4^7 \times 4^7$ (g) $8^0 \times 8 \times 8^2$ (h) $6^0 \times 6^2 \times 6^9$

2 Use the fact that $2^{10} = 1024$ to work these out.

(a) 2^9 (b) 2^8 (c) 2^{11} (d) 2^{12}

3 The table shows some powers of 3.

3^4	3^5	3^6	3^7	3^8	3^9	3^{10}	3^{11}
81	243	729	2187	6561	19683	59049	177147

Use the table to evaluate these.

(a) 81×243 (b) 81×2187 (c) 729×243 (d) 243^2

4 Simplify each of these.

(a) $a \times a \times a$ (b) $a^3 \times a^2$ (c) $a^5 \times a^5$ (d) $a^3 \times a$

(e) $a^2 \times a^3 \times a^4$ (f) $a \times a^5 \times a$ (g) $a \times a^3 \times a^2$ (h) $a^4 \times a^4 \times a^4$

5 Simplify each of these.

(a) $(3^4)^2$ (b) $(2^5)^3$ (c) $(a^2)^3$ (d) $(b^1)^3$ (e) $(c^0)^2$

6 Simplify each of these.

(a) $2a \times 3a^3$ (b) $e^2 \times 5e^3$ (c) $3f \times 2f^8$ (d) $3h^5 \times 7h^3$

(e) $5d^4 \times 2d^5$ (f) $3g^2 \times 5g^6$ (g) $2p \times 3p^2 \times 4p^3$ (h) $3m \times 2m^7 \times m^3$

7 Copy and complete these multiplication walls.

(a)
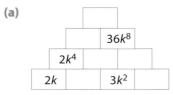

(b)
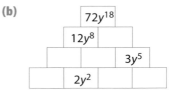

8 Simplify these.

(a) $(2c^2)^3$ (b) $(3k^0)^4$ (c) $(5b^4)^3$ (d) $(2v^3)^5$

*9 Write 8^4 as a power of 2.

*10 Write a third of 9^{10} as a power of 3.

D Dividing powers
E Dividing expressions with powers

1 Write the answers to these using indices.

(a) $5^8 \div 5^3$ (b) $4^7 \div 4^4$ (c) $6^3 \div 6$ (d) $3^5 \div 3^2$

(e) $\dfrac{2^7}{2^3}$ (f) $\dfrac{5^6}{5^0}$ (g) $\dfrac{4^5}{4}$ (h) $\dfrac{7^8}{7^7}$

2 Write the answers to these using indices.

(a) $\dfrac{3^5 \times 3^4}{3^2}$ (b) $\dfrac{5^3 \times 5^2}{5^4}$ (c) $\dfrac{(6^2)^3}{6^4}$ (d) $\dfrac{7^5 \times 7^2}{7^4 \times 7}$

3 Find the value of w in each of the following expressions.

(a) $7^5 \div 7^2 = 7^w$ (b) $\dfrac{4^6}{4^w} = 4$ (c) $\dfrac{3 \times 3^3}{3^4} = 3^w$ (d) $\dfrac{b^9}{b^w} = b^2$

4 Simplify each of these.

(a) $d^5 \div d^3$ (b) $\dfrac{e^7}{(e^3)^2}$ (c) $\dfrac{b^4 \times b^2}{b^3}$ (d) $\dfrac{s^3 \times s^4}{s^6 \times s}$ (e) $\dfrac{t^5 \times t^2}{t^2 \times t}$

 5

6^2	6^3	6^4	6^5	6^6	6^7	6^8
36	216	1296	7776	46 656	279 936	1 679 616

Use the powers of 6 in the table above to evaluate these.

(a) $\dfrac{1296}{36}$ (b) $\dfrac{46\,656}{7776}$ (c) $\dfrac{279\,936}{1296}$

(d) $\dfrac{1\,679\,616}{46\,656}$ (e) $\dfrac{216 \times 7776}{279\,936}$ (f) $\dfrac{1296^2}{216}$

6 Simplify these.

(a) $\dfrac{7b^5}{b^2}$ (b) $\dfrac{9c^6}{3c}$ (c) $\dfrac{20n^4}{4n^2}$ (d) $\dfrac{16m^5}{2m^4}$ (e) $\dfrac{30s^8}{5s^4}$

7 Simplify these by cancelling.

(a) $\dfrac{3^3}{3^5}$ (b) $\dfrac{2^5}{2^{10}}$ (c) $\dfrac{5}{5^6}$ (d) $\dfrac{4^3}{4^4}$

8 Simplify these by cancelling.

(a) $\dfrac{k^4}{k^8}$ (b) $\dfrac{m^3}{m^7}$ (c) $\dfrac{t^5}{t^6}$ (d) $\dfrac{s}{s^4}$

9 Simplify these by cancelling.

(a) $\dfrac{4a^3}{a^5}$ (b) $\dfrac{2c^7}{6c^2}$ (c) $\dfrac{15d^8}{10d^3}$ (d) $\dfrac{e}{3e^5}$

(e) $\dfrac{10k^3}{15k}$ (f) $\dfrac{6q^2 \times 3q^4}{15q^2}$ (g) $\dfrac{2r \times 2r^2}{10r^8}$ (h) $\dfrac{9p}{2p^2 \times 6p^3}$

F Negative indices

1 Copy and complete these.

(a) $5^{-3} = \dfrac{1}{5^{\blacksquare}}$

(b) $\dfrac{1}{3^2} = 3^{\blacksquare}$

(c) $\dfrac{1}{4} = \dfrac{1}{2^{\blacksquare}} = 2^{\blacksquare}$

(d) $\dfrac{1}{27} = \dfrac{1}{3^{\blacksquare}} = 3^{\blacksquare}$

(e) $\dfrac{1}{64} = 4^{\blacksquare}$

(f) $\dfrac{1}{10\,000} = 10^{\blacksquare}$

2 Find the missing number in each statement below.

(a) $\dfrac{1}{8} = 2^{\blacksquare}$

(b) $\blacksquare^{-2} = \dfrac{1}{9}$

(c) $\dfrac{1}{5} = 5^{\blacksquare}$

(d) $4^{-2} = \dfrac{1}{\blacksquare}$

3 2^{-4} is equivalent to the fraction $\frac{1}{16}$.

Write the following as fractions.

(a) 4^{-1} (b) 2^{-5} (c) 3^{-2} (d) 5^{-2} (e) 10^{-3}

4 Put the following numbers in order of size, starting with the smallest.

(a) 2^{-3} 10^{-1} $\dfrac{1}{9}$ $\dfrac{1}{5^2}$

(b) 4^{-1} 3^{-2} $\dfrac{1}{2}$ $\dfrac{1}{2^3}$

5 $10^{-2} = \dfrac{1}{10^2} = \dfrac{1}{100} = 0.01$ as a decimal.

Write the following as decimals.

(a) 10^{-1} (b) 10^{-3} (c) 10^{-5} (d) 10^{-8} (e) 10^{-4}

6 Write the following as decimals.

(a) 8^{-1} (b) 5^{-2} (c) 2^{-3} (d) 16^{-1} (e) 4^{-3}

7 Write the following as decimals correct to three significant figures.

(a) 7^{-1} (b) 6^{-2} (c) 9^{-2} (d) 11^{-1} (e) 5×3^{-2}

8 Write these in fractional form.

(a) x^{-2} (b) z^{-4} (c) w^{-1} (d) n^{-2} (e) h^{-7}

9 Solve these.

(a) $11^{-1} = \dfrac{1}{x}$

(b) $x^{-2} = 0.01$

(c) $7^x = \frac{1}{7}$

(d) $9^x = 1$

(e) $x^{-2} = \frac{1}{64}$

(f) $x^{-3} = 1$

(g) $3^x = \frac{1}{81}$

(h) $10^x = 0.000\,000\,1$

*10 Evaluate $\left(\frac{1}{2}\right)^{-2}$.

*11 Evaluate $\left(\frac{3}{2}\right)^{-3}$ and write the result as a fraction.

*12 Solve these.

(a) $\left(\frac{1}{3}\right)^p = 27$

(b) $n^{-2} = 16$

(c) $m^{-4} = \frac{81}{16}$

(d) $x^{-2} = 2.25$

G Extending the rules to negative indices

1 Write the answer to each of these as a single power.

(a) $4^4 \times 4^{-2}$ (b) $7^{-3} \times 7^5$ (c) $2^{-5} \times 2^3$ (d) $3^5 \times 3^{-5}$

(e) $6^{-6} \times 6^3$ (f) $8^{-2} \times 8$ (g) $5^{-3} \times 5^{-2} \times 5$ (h) $2^5 \times 2^{-3} \times 2^{-2}$

2 Write the answer to each of these as a single power.

(a) $4^3 \div 4^5$ (b) $\dfrac{3^2}{3^3}$ (c) $2 \div 2^4$ (d) $\dfrac{5}{5^3}$

(e) $\dfrac{7^4}{7^5}$ (f) $9 \div 9^5$ (g) $\dfrac{6^4}{6^6}$ (h) $2^3 \div 2^9$

3 Simplify each of these.

(a) $s^4 \times s^{-3}$ (b) $h^{-2} \times h^5$ (c) $k^4 \times k^{-4}$ (d) $x^2 \times x^{-7}$

(e) $n^{-5} \times n^{-1}$ (f) $m^4 \div m^7$ (g) $\dfrac{x^2}{x^6}$ (h) $\dfrac{d}{d^5}$

4 Write each of these as a single power.

(a) $(3^{-2})^3$ (b) $(2^3)^{-4}$ (c) $(7^5)^{-1}$ (d) $(x^5)^{-4}$ (e) $(k^{-7})^{-2}$

5 Find the value of n in each statement.

(a) $2^5 \times 2^n = 2^2$ (b) $7^{-5} \times 7^n = 7^{-2}$ (c) $5^{-2} \times 5^n = 5^{-5}$

(d) $\dfrac{2^3}{2^n} = 2^{-2}$ (e) $\dfrac{2^n}{2^5} = 2^{-9}$ (f) $(3^{-3})^n = 3^{-6}$

6 Simplify each of these.

(a) $3x^3 \times 5x^{-2}$ (b) $2p^5 \times 4p^{-2}$ (c) $3k^2 \times 2k^{-4}$ (d) $\dfrac{5a^3}{a^8}$

(e) $\dfrac{2y}{y^5}$ (f) $\dfrac{5x^7}{10x^8}$ (g) $\dfrac{12h}{4h^7}$ (h) $\dfrac{6m^3}{8m^4}$

7 Write each of these as a single power.

(a) $2^2 \div 2^{-4}$ (b) $3^{-5} \div 3^{-7}$ (c) $5^{-4} \div 5^{-1}$ (d) $\dfrac{x}{x^{-3}}$ (e) $\dfrac{h^{-3}}{h^{-2}}$

8 Copy and complete these multiplication grids.

(a)

$\times$		5^{-2}	
		5^{-6}	
5^2			5^2
5^{-1}	5^2		

(b)

$\times$		y^3	y^{-4}
	1		y^{-1}
1			
		1	

9 Simplify $\dfrac{15k^{-3}}{10k^{-8}}$.

11 Surveys and experiments

B Surveys

1 A questionnaire for college students is being designed.

(a) Which of these two questions is better? Explain why.

A

What was your main means of transport to college this morning?
Walk or cycle ☐   Public transport ☐   Private car ☐

B

How did you travel to college this morning?
_____

(b) Criticise this question and suggest a better version.

How many times have you been away on holiday in the past 12 months?
0 ☐   1 ☐   2 ☐   3 ☐   4 or more ☐

2 A survey of mobile phone use in a college produced the results shown in the table.

Draw a suitable diagram to illustrate the data.

Network	Males	Females
Virgin	14	9
O$_2$	16	20
T-mobile	12	10
Orange	8	11

C Experiments

A group of 15 students attended a workshop on keyboard skills. Afterwards each student was timed typing a paragraph and entering data into a spreadsheet. 15 students who had not been at the workshop were also timed. The times in seconds are given below.

Students who attended the workshop

Paragraph	28 34 37 25 29 26 33 39 26 38 23 29 26 34 38
Spreadsheet	26 36 32 28 31 31 35 37 30 34 25 27 27 38 34

Students who did not attend the workshop

Paragraph	27 37 38 42 38 33 33 28 32 28 34 35 44 34 37
Spreadsheet	38 35 45 30 33 40 34 37 38 41 27 43 43 26 33

1 Write a short report comparing the performances of the two groups.

2 Write a short report on whether there was any link between paragraph and spreadsheet times.

12 Speed, distance and time

A Calculating speed

1 Calculate the average speed of each of the following.
   State the units of your answers.

   (a) A bus that goes 38 miles in 2 hours   (b) A car that goes 117 miles in 3 hours

   (c) A train that goes 48 km in $\frac{1}{2}$ hour   (d) A dog that runs 200 m in 40 seconds

2 A plane flying at constant speed travels 450 km in $1\frac{1}{2}$ hours.
   What is the speed of the plane in km/h?

3 Kirsti recorded her mileometer readings during a journey.

Start	Break	End
32 403	32 518	32 593

   (a) She drove for $2\frac{1}{2}$ hours before her break. What was her average speed?

   (b) She drove for $1\frac{1}{2}$ hours after her break. What was her average speed after her break?

   (c) What was her average driving speed for the whole journey?

4 A train left for a 70 mile journey at 10:15 and arrived at its destination at 11:30.
   It started its return journey at 11:40, arriving back at 13:25.

   (a) What was the average speed of the train for the outward journey?

   (b) What was the average speed of the train for the return journey?

B Distance–time graphs

1 Describe each of these journeys fully.

(a)
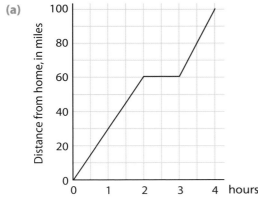

(b)
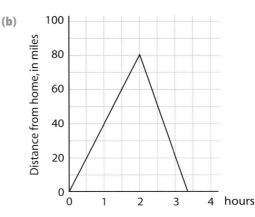

2 Randeep drives from Birmingham to Liverpool. Barry does the same journey by coach. This graph shows their journeys.

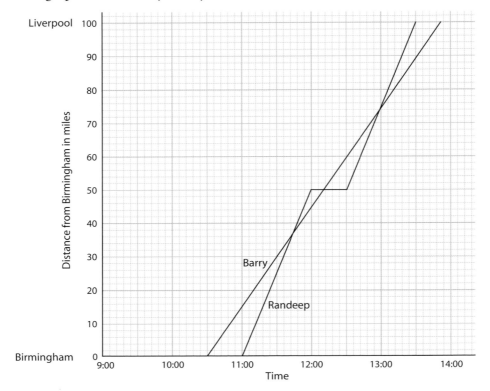

(a) How far is it from Birmingham to Liverpool?

(b) At what time did Barry leave Birmingham?

(c) How long did it take him to travel to Liverpool?

(d) At what speed did he travel to Liverpool?

(e) Randeep stopped on the way. For how long did he stop?

(f) At what time did Randeep first overtake Barry?

(g) How far apart were they at 12:30?

(h) At what speed did Randeep drive after his break?

(i) How much later than Randeep did Barry arrive in Liverpool?

3 Make a copy of the axes above on graph paper.

(a) Sasha leaves Liverpool at 10:00 and drives towards Birmingham at 40 m.p.h. Draw and label the graph of her journey.

(b) Lee leaves Birmingham at 11:30 and drives towards Liverpool at 60 m.p.h. for $1\frac{1}{2}$ hours. He stops for half an hour and then drives the rest of the way to Liverpool at 40 m.p.h. Draw and label the graph of his journey.

(c) At what time do Sasha and Lee pass each other?

(d) How far are they from Birmingham when they pass?

4 The graph shows the journey of a person walking to a village shop and a cyclist doing the same journey to the shop and then returning.

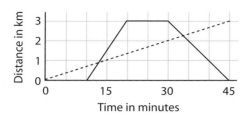

(a) Calculate the speed of the cyclist on the return journey.

(b) What is the difference, in km/h, between the speeds of the cyclist and the walker when the cyclist overtakes the walker on the way to the shop?

C Calculating distance and time
D Mixing units

1 Sue cycles at 32 km/h for 2 hours. How far does she travel?

2 A dolphin swims at a steady speed of 30 km/h. How long does it take to swim 75 km?

3 A hot-air balloon takes off at 7:30 and lands at 9:00. It travels at 4 m.p.h. How far does it travel in this time?

4 A train travels at a speed of 80 m.p.h. How long does it take to travel 60 miles?

5 A bus travels 5 miles in 20 minutes. Calculate its average speed in miles per hour.

6 A helicopter flies at a speed of 180 km/h. How far does it fly in 10 minutes?

7 An ostrich can run at a speed of 18 m/s. At this speed, how far does it travel in

   (a) 10 seconds   (b) 30 seconds   (c) 1 minute   (d) 5 minutes

8 A boat travels at 24 km/h. How far does it travel in

   (a) 30 minutes   (b) 20 minutes   (c) 5 minutes   (d) 15 **seconds**

9 Dave drives for $2\frac{1}{2}$ hours at an average speed of 52 m.p.h. His mileometer reads 13 584 at the start of his journey. What is his mileometer reading at the end of the journey?

10 Martin travelled for 15 minutes at 24 km/h then for 20 minutes at 45 km/h.

   (a) How far did he travel altogether?

   (b) What was his average speed for the whole journey?

11 Traffic in London was travelling at an average speed of 3 m.p.h.
Jody's taxi driver told her that her destination was 2 miles away.
Jody can walk at 4 m.p.h. and the route for walking was only $1\frac{1}{2}$ miles.

How much quicker would it be for Jody to walk, rather than stay in the taxi?

E Time on a calculator

1 A car travels a distance of 37 miles in 48 minutes.

  (a) Change 48 minutes into decimals of an hour.

  (b) Calculate the average speed of the car in m.p.h.

2 Sam walks a distance of 10 km in 1 hour 25 minutes.
Calculate her average speed in km/h, to one decimal place.

3 Find the times taken, in hours and minutes, for these journeys.

  (a) 38 miles at 15 m.p.h.   **(b)** 448 km at 105 km/h   **(c)** 28 miles at 70 m.p.h.

4 A plane is flying at a speed of 260 m.p.h. How far does it go in 55 minutes?

5 Asafa Powell broke the world 100 m sprint record on 14 June 2005.
His time was 9.77 seconds.
Calculate his speed in m/s, to one decimal place.

6 The Moon moves around the Earth at an average speed of 3700 km/h.
How far does it travel in one day?

7 The Japanese bullet train can travel at an average speed of 206 km/h.
It takes $2\frac{1}{2}$ hours to travel from Tokyo to Osaka.
Calculate the distance from Tokyo to Osaka.

8 During the first trial in July 1900, a Zeppelin flew 6 km in 17 minutes.
Calculate the speed of the Zeppelin in km/h to one decimal place.

9 The common snail travels at 0.03 m.p.h.

  (a) How long, in hours and minutes, would it take a common snail to cover a mile?

  (b) How far would a snail be able to travel in 25 minutes?

10 Kath cycles 50 miles at an average speed of 12 m.p.h.
She begins her journey at 1:30 p.m.
At what time does she finish her journey?

11 Anita drove at an average speed of 30 m.p.h. for 10 miles and then
at an average speed of 50 m.p.h. for 15 miles.

Calculate her average speed for the whole journey.
Give your answer to an appropriate degree of accuracy.

13 Volume, surface area and density

A Volume of a cuboid

1 Find the volume of each cuboid, giving your answers to 2 s.f.

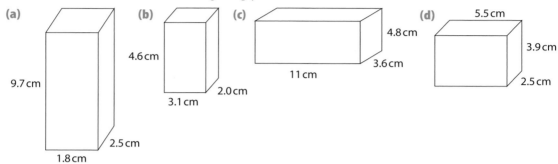

(a) 9.7 cm, 2.5 cm, 1.8 cm

(b) 4.6 cm, 3.1 cm, 2.0 cm

(c) 4.8 cm, 11 cm, 3.6 cm

(d) 5.5 cm, 3.9 cm, 2.5 cm

2 These cuboids all have the same volume.
Find the missing measurements.

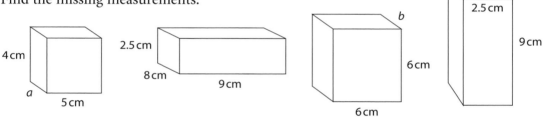

4 cm, 5 cm, a

2.5 cm, 8 cm, 9 cm

b, 6 cm, 6 cm

2.5 cm, c, 9 cm

3 A certain cuboid has a volume of 192 cm³.
Give three different possible combinations of its length, width and height.

B Volume of a prism

1 Find the volume of each prism, rounding to the nearest 0.1 cm³ where necessary.

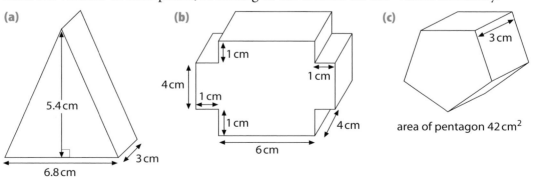

(a) 5.4 cm, 6.8 cm, 3 cm

(b) 1 cm, 1 cm, 4 cm, 1 cm, 1 cm, 4 cm, 6 cm

(c) 3 cm, area of pentagon 42 cm²

2 A desk-tidy has the shape of a prism with a trapezium for its cross-section.
Find the volume of the desk-tidy.

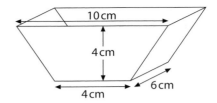

3 A block of fondant icing with volume 250 cm³ is spread evenly over the rectangular top of a cake, measuring 32 cm by 18 cm.
How thick will the icing be?

4 Concrete for a factory floor has to be laid to a depth of 12 cm.
What area would a 18 m³ load of liquid concrete cover?

C Volume of a cylinder

1 Find the volume of each of these cylinders, giving your answers to 3 s.f.

   (a) Base radius = 2.5 cm, length = 14 cm

   (b) Base radius = 7.4 m, length = 0.8 m

2 A cylindrical sewage tank has a diameter of 21 metres and is 7 metres deep.
What is the volume of the tank?

3 A cylindrical block of wood has a radius of 5.6 cm and a volume of 2000 cm³.
What is the height of the block, correct to the nearest 0.1 cm?

4 A cylindrical can of hair spray holds 770 cm³. The can is 16.5 cm tall. Find the radius.

5 All of these cylinders have the same volume.
Find the missing measurements.

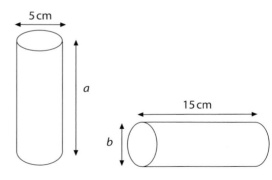

6

This toilet roll has height 11 cm and diameter 12 cm.

The cardboard tube has an internal diameter of 4.5 cm and thickness of 1 mm.

   (a) Find the volume of paper on the roll.

   (b) There are 280 sheets on the roll which are 12.4 cm by 11 cm.
   Calculate the thickness of each sheet.

D Surface area

1 (a) By measuring, find the total surface area of this net.

(b) What shape will it make when folded together?

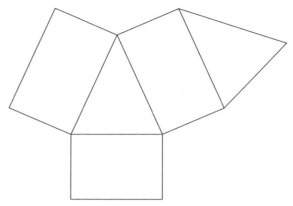

2 Find the surface area of each of these prisms. Sketch nets if you need to.

(a)

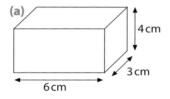

4 cm
3 cm
6 cm

(b)

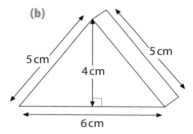

5 cm
5 cm
4 cm
6 cm

(c)

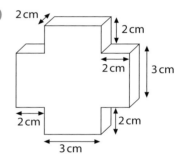

2 cm
2 cm
2 cm
3 cm
2 cm
2 cm
3 cm

3 Calculate the total surface area of each of these cylinders.

(a)

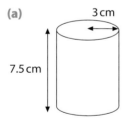

3 cm
7.5 cm

(b)

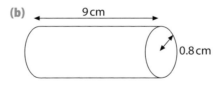

9 cm
0.8 cm

(c)

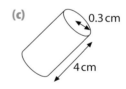

0.3 cm
4 cm

E Density

1 Find **(i)** the volume and **(ii)** the density of each of these objects.

(a) A block of hardwood measuring 10 cm by 10 cm and 50 cm long which weighs 4.2 kg

(b) A foam brick measuring 6 cm by 10 cm by 21 cm and weighing 85 g

(c) A solid cylinder of glass 8 cm tall with diameter 10 cm and mass 1.4 kg

2 An ingot of gold has a mass of 350 g. The density of gold is 19.3 g/cm^3. What is the volume of the ingot?

3 This table shows the density of some metals.
Find the mass of each of these objects.

Material	Density
Aluminium	$2.6\,g/cm^3$
Tin	$7.3\,g/cm^3$
Bronze	$8.8\,g/cm^3$

(a) A sheet of aluminium 80 cm long
by 50 cm wide and 0.5 cm thick

(b) A block of tin 5 cm by 3 cm by 2 cm

(c) A bronze coin with diameter 1.6 cm and thickness 0.2 cm

4 A statue has mass 28 kg and is made of stone with density $3.2\,g/cm^3$.
It is immersed in water in a tank with vertical sides and with
a base measuring 85 cm by 40 cm.

By how much will the water level in the tank rise when the statue is put in?

F Units of volume and liquid measure

1 (a) Find the volume of each
of these prisms in cm^3.

(i)

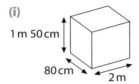

(ii)

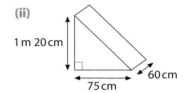

(b) Change the volumes in (a) into m^3.

2 A tank in the shape of a cylinder has a radius of 1.6 m and a depth of 2.5 m.
Calculate the volume of the tank in   (a) m^3 (b) cm^3

3 Change these volumes in cm^3 into m^3.

(a) $7\,000\,000\,cm^3$ (b) $24\,000\,000\,cm^3$ (c) $3\,870\,000\,cm^3$ (d) $50\,000\,cm^3$

4 A box has a volume of $12.8\,cm^3$. What is this volume in mm^3?

5 A bucket can be filled with $12\,000\,cm^3$ of sand.
How many buckets of sand can you get from 1 cubic metre of sand?

6 A beaker in the shape of a cylinder has a radius of 6 cm and a height of 20 cm.

(a) Find the capacity of the beaker, correct to the nearest millilitre.

(b) What is this capacity in litres?

7 An tank contains $2.5\,m^3$ of oil.
How many 5 litre containers can be filled from the tank?

8 A water container in the shape of a cylinder holds 1 litre of water.
It has a diameter of 8 cm. What is its height?

*9 A cylindrical container holds exactly 1 litre of liquid.
Its diameter is the same as its height. What is its diameter?

14 Cumulative frequency

You need graph paper for sections C, D and E.

B Cumulative frequency tables

1 A sample of cooks were asked how long they boiled greens for.
   The results are shown in the table.

   (a) How many cooks boiled greens for 15 minutes or less?

   (b) How many boiled greens for 25 minutes or less?

   (c) How many cooks were questioned?

Time (t min)	Frequency
$0 < t \le 5$	10
$5 < t \le 10$	15
$10 < t \le 15$	13
$15 < t \le 20$	3
$20 < t \le 25$	1
$25 < t \le 30$	1

2 Make a cumulative frequency table for each of these.

(a)

Test result (r)	Frequency
$0 < r \le 20$	3
$20 < r \le 40$	7
$40 < r \le 60$	20
$60 < r \le 80$	32
$80 < r \le 100$	10

(b)

Weekly wage (£w)	Frequency
$150 < w \le 160$	5
$160 < w \le 170$	10
$170 < w \le 180$	23
$180 < w \le 190$	16
$190 < w \le 200$	8

3 This cumulative frequency table gives information about the age distribution
   of the population of a country.

Age (a years)	$a \le 20$	$a \le 40$	$a \le 60$	$a \le 80$	$a \le 100$
Cumulative frequency (in millions)	9	21	35	41	44

   (a) What is the total population of the country?

   (b) How many people are in the following age intervals?

   (ii) $20 < a \le 40$ (ii) $60 < a \le 100$

   (c) Copy and complete this frequency table for the data.

Age (a years)	Frequency
$0 < a \le 20$	9
$20 < a \le 40$	
$40 < a \le 60$	
$60 < a \le 80$	
$80 < a \le 100$	

c Cumulative frequency graphs

1 A mouse breeder likes to weigh all his mice every week as a check on their health. Here is the cumulative frequency graph of his results for one week.

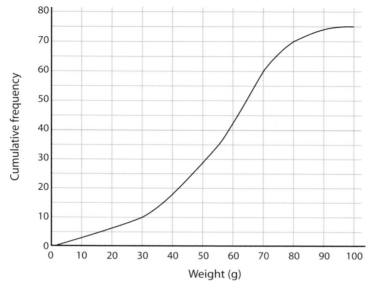

(a) Use the graph to estimate how many mice weigh up to

(i) 25 g   (ii) 45 g   (iii) 65 g   (iv) 85 g

(b) Estimate the percentage of mice that weigh

(i) up to 25 g   (ii) up to 45 g   (iii) over 65 g   (iv) over 45 g

(v) between 50 g and 90 g

(c) Copy and complete this statement:

'80% of the mice weigh ... g or less.'

2 This table gives information about the midday temperature at a holiday resort each day for a year.

(a) Make a table of cumulative frequencies.

(b) Draw a cumulative frequency graph.

(c) Estimate the number of days for which the temperature was between 15 °C and 25 °C.

(d) Estimate the percentage of the days that had a temperature over 23 °C.

Temperature (T °C)	Frequency
$^{-}10 < T \leq 0$	3
$0 < T \leq 10$	83
$10 < T \leq 20$	196
$20 < T \leq 30$	80
$30 < T \leq 40$	3

D Median, quartiles and interquartile range

1 This is the cumulative frequency graph for the marks of 160 students.

From the graph estimate

(a) the median mark

(b) the lower quartile

(c) the upper quartile

(d) the interquartile range

(e) the pass mark if three-quarters of the students passed

(f) the number of students achieving more than 30 marks

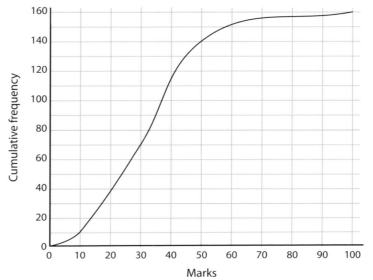

2 Here are the heights of some pupils in a school.

Height (h cm)	Frequency
$140 < h \leq 145$	3
$145 < h \leq 150$	5
$150 < h \leq 155$	10
$155 < h \leq 160$	12
$160 < h \leq 165$	15
$165 < h \leq 170$	6
$170 < h \leq 175$	3
$175 < h \leq 180$	2

(a) Make a cumulative frequency table.

(b) Draw a cumulative frequency graph.

(c) Use the graph to estimate

(i) the median

(ii) the quartiles

(iii) the interquartile range

3 The speeds in m.p.h. of 200 cars travelling along a particular road were measured. The results are shown in this cumulative frequency table.

Speed (s m.p.h.)	$s \leq 20$	$s \leq 25$	$s \leq 30$	$s \leq 35$	$s \leq 40$	$s \leq 45$	$s \leq 50$	$s \leq 55$	$s \leq 60$
Cumulative frequency	1	7	16	30	64	110	167	188	200

Draw a cumulative frequency graph and use it to estimate the median and quartiles.

E Box-and-whisker plots

1 (a) Draw a box-and-whisker plot to show this information about the weights of 60 family bags of crisps.

> A quarter of the bags weighed 142 g or less, the lightest being 123 g.
> A quarter of the bags weighed 151 g or more, the heaviest being 163 g.
> The median weight was 148 g.

   (b) What is the interquartile range of the weights?

2 People working for a company may be part-time or full-time.
Full-time workers may have opportunities to work overtime.

The box-and-whisker plots below show the hours worked by men and women in a typical working week.

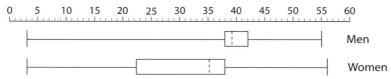

Write a couple of sentences comparing the hours worked by men and women.

3 These graphs show the results of two tests taken by the same group.

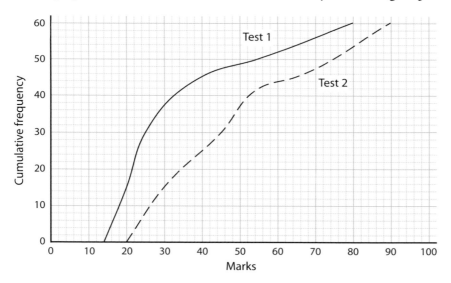

   (a) Find the median and quartiles for each test.
   (b) Draw two box-and-whisker plots, one for each test.
   (c) Write down the interquartile range for each test.
   (d) Write a couple of sentences comparing the two sets of results.
   (e) If the pass mark was 55 marks, how many passed each test?

Mixed practice 2

You need squared paper and graph paper.

1 Work out the value of $3^n - 1$ when $n = 2$.

2 On squared paper, draw a set of axes, each numbered from $^-5$ to 10.
Plot and join the points $(^-2, 2)$, $(^-2, 4)$, $(0, 4)$ and $(^-1, 2)$.
Label the shape A.

  (a) Draw the enlargement of shape A with scale factor 2 and centre $(0, 0)$.
Label the image B.

  (b) Plot the points $(4, ^-2)$, $(4, 4)$, $(10, 4)$ and $(7, ^-2)$ and join them up.
Label the quadrilateral C.

  (c) Describe fully the transformation that maps shape A to shape C.

3 Sadia is carrying out a survey about food in the school canteen.
She asks this question.

Should there be more vegetarian options, which are more healthy than meat?   Yes/No

Say what is wrong with this question and suggest a way of improving it.

4 (a) A plane travels for $4\frac{3}{4}$ hours at 392 m.p.h. How far does it go?

  (b) Kylie drives 295 miles at an average speed of 50 m.p.h.
How long does her journey take in hours and minutes?

5 The table shows the weights of 110 schoolbags.

Weight (w kg)	$0.5 < w \le 1$	$1 < w \le 1.5$	$1.5 < w \le 2$	$2 < w \le 2.5$	$2.5 < w \le 3$	$3 < w \le 3.5$
Frequency	7	16	39	28	18	2

  (a) Copy and complete the cumulative frequency table below.

Weight (kg)	$w \le 0.5$	$w \le 1$	$w \le 1.5$	$w \le 2$	$w \le 2.5$	$w \le 3$	$w \le 3.5$
Cumulative frequency	0						

  (b) On graph paper, draw a cumulative frequency graph.

  (c) Estimate how many of the schoolbags weigh less than 1.75 kg.

  (d) Estimate the percentage of the bags that weigh more than 2.8 kg.

  (e) Use your graph to estimate

    (i) the median weight   **(ii)** the interquartile range

  (f) Draw a box-and-whisker plot.

6 Solve these equations.

  (a) $x^6 = 64$ **(b)** $9^x = 1$ **(c)** $2^x = \frac{1}{8}$ **(d)** $5^x = 0.2$

7 This solid cylinder is made from aluminium.

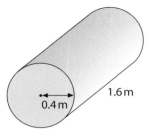

(a) (i) Calculate its volume in m³, correct to three significant figures.

(ii) Write down this volume in cm³.

(iii) The density of aluminium is 2.7 g/cm³. To the nearest kg, find the mass of this cylinder.

(b) Calculate the surface area of the cylinder in m², correct to three significant figures.

8 Write each of these as a single power.

(a) $7^{10} \div 7^2$ (b) $9^5 \times 9^{-3}$ (c) $\dfrac{4^5 \times 4^4}{4^3}$ (d) $\dfrac{(3^3)^2}{3^7}$

9 On squared paper, draw a set of axes, each numbered from ⁻6 to 6.
Plot and join the points (2, 2), (2, 5), (5, 3) and (5, 2).
Label the shape A.

(a) (i) Draw the image of A after reflection in the line with equation $y = 1$. Label it B.

(ii) Draw the image of B after a rotation through 180° about the point (1, 1). Label it C.

(iii) What single transformation maps shape C back on to shape A?

(b) (i) Draw the image of C after a rotation 90° anticlockwise about (0, 0) Label it D.

(ii) Draw the image of D after the translation $\begin{bmatrix} 3 \\ -1 \end{bmatrix}$. Label the image E.

(iii) What single transformation maps shape B on to shape E?

10 Simplify each of these expressions.

(a) $6k \times 5k^3$ (b) $\dfrac{a^3}{a^4}$ (c) $\dfrac{16b^7}{8b^2}$ (d) $\dfrac{15m}{25m^4}$ (e) $(2x^{-3})^3$

11 (a) A car travelling at constant speed takes 5 seconds to travel 100 m. Find the speed of the car in kilometres per hour.

(b) Another car travels at 90 km/h. How long, in seconds, does it take to travel 100 m?

12 A skip is made in the shape of a prism whose cross-section is a trapezium.

How many litres of water will it contain when it is full?

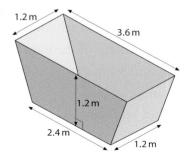

✗ *13 Solve the equation $x^{-2} = 2.25$.

15 Working with expressions

A Collecting like terms

level 6

1 Simplify the following by collecting like terms.

(a) $p^2 + 3p + 2p^2 - 4p$

(b) $4x^2 + 2x - x^2 - 1$

(c) $7y + 5y^2 - 2 + 4y$

(d) $8n^2 - 4n - 3n^2 + 3$

(e) $5l - 6 - 3l^2 + 7l^2$

(f) $k^2 - 6k + 3k^2 + 10k + 1$

2 Find the value of each expression when $x = 3$.

(a) $x^3 + x^2 + 7 - x^3$

(b) $x^2 + 3x - 2x$

(c) $6x^2 - 5x^2 + 2x + 2$

(d) $x^3 + x^2 + x - x^2 + 5$

3

A $m^2 + m^3$ **B** $2m - m^3$ **C** $4m^2 - 2m - 2$ **D** $2 - m^2$

(a) Find pairs of the above expressions that add to give

(i) $m^3 + 2$

(ii) $m^2 + 2m$

(iii) $3m^2 - 2m$

(iv) $4m^2 - m^3 - 2$

(b) Find three of the expressions that add to give $2m + 2$.

B Multiplying and dividing expressions
C Factorising expressions

1 Multiply out the brackets in these.

(a) $x(x + 6)$

(b) $4(3a + 5)$

(c) $4m(2 - m)$

(d) $2n(3n + 1)$

(e) $4k^2(3k - 2)$

(f) $3p(p^3 - p^2)$

(g) $4w^2(2 + 3w^2)$

(h) $x^3(4x^2 - x)$

2 Find the expressions missing from these statements.

(a) $n(\blacksquare\blacksquare\blacksquare) = n^2 - 3n$

(b) $3x(\blacksquare\blacksquare\blacksquare) = 6x - 9x^2$

(c) $4p(\blacksquare\blacksquare\blacksquare) = 4p^2 - 8p^3$

(d) $2k(\blacksquare\blacksquare\blacksquare) = 6k + 2k^4$

3 Simplify each of these.

(a) $\dfrac{6n - 9}{3}$

(b) $\dfrac{2p^2 - 6p}{p}$

(c) $\dfrac{2x^2 - 6x}{2x}$

(d) $\dfrac{9k^3 + 12k^4}{3k^2}$

4 Find the missing expressions.

(a) $\dfrac{\blacksquare\blacksquare\blacksquare}{4} = 2x + 5$

(b) $\dfrac{\blacksquare\blacksquare\blacksquare}{n} = n - 5$

(c) $\dfrac{\blacksquare\blacksquare\blacksquare}{2m^2} = m + 5$

5

4		n		$3n$		n^2		$3n - 2$		$n - 1$

Find pairs of the above expressions that multiply to give

(a) $n^2 - n$ (b) $4n^2$ (c) $3n^2 - 2n$ (d) $3n^2 - 3n$

(e) $12n - 8$ (f) $9n^2 - 6n$ (g) $3n^3 - 2n^2$ (h) $n^3 - n^2$

6 Factorise each of these.

(a) $4x + 8$ (b) $a^2 - 3a$ (c) $3k^3 - 2k$ (d) $12g - g^2$ (e) $3y^2 - 6$

7 Find the missing expressions in these statements.

(a) $4p(\blacksquare\blacksquare\blacksquare) = 4p^2 + 12p$ (b) $9n(\blacksquare\blacksquare\blacksquare) = 18n^2 + 9n$

(c) $3x(\blacksquare\blacksquare\blacksquare) = 6x^3 + 9x$ (d) $y^2(\blacksquare\blacksquare\blacksquare) = 4y^4 + 3y^3$

8 Factorise each of these completely.

(a) $8x^2 + 10x$ (b) $3d^2 + 15d$ (c) $4y + 12y^2$ (d) $10h^2 - 25h^3$

*9 (a) Factorise $5n + 10$.

(b) Explain how the factorisation tells you that $5n + 10$ will be a multiple of 5 for any integer n.

D Dealing with more than one letter

1 Find the value of each expression when $x = 3$ and $y = 4$.

(a) $2xy + y$ (b) $3y^2 - x$ (c) $2x^2 + y^2 - 2$ (d) $4x + 2y^2 - 3y$

(e) $(xy)^2$ (f) x^2y (g) xy^2 (h) x^2y^2

2 Find the value of each expression when $a = 2$, $b = 5$ and $c = {}^-6$.

(a) $2a + 3b + c$ (b) $ab + bc$ (c) $4ab - c^2$

(d) $ab^2 - 3c + b$ (e) $\dfrac{bc}{a}$ (f) $\dfrac{2b + a}{c}$

3 Simplify the following expressions by collecting like terms.

(a) $3n + m + 4n - 3m$ (b) $mn + 3n^2 + 3mn + 2 + 6n^2$ (c) $8m - n^2 + 4m + 3n^2$

4

A	**B**	**C**	**D**
$a^2 - b$	$2a + b$	$4b - b^2$	$2a^2 - b^2$

Find pairs of the above expressions that add to give

(a) $3a^2 - b^2 - b$ (b) $a^2 + 2a$ (c) $2a + 5b - b^2$ (d) $2a^2 - 2b^2 + 4b$

5 Find the result of each multiplication in its simplest form.

(a) $a \times 3b$ (b) $2x \times 5y$ (c) $2k \times 3m$ (d) $4n \times 3p$

(e) $5x \times 4y$ (f) $3x^2 \times 4y$ (g) $4ab \times 3b^2$ (h) $2xy^2 \times 4x^2y^4$

6 Find the missing expression in each statement.

(a) $3x \times \blacksquare = 12xy$ (b) $\blacksquare \times 6m^2n = 18m^3n^2$ (c) $4p^2q \times \blacksquare = 20p^5q^4$

7

| $3x$ | $4y$ | $5xy$ | $4x^2$ | $3x^2y$ | x^3y |

Find pairs of the above expressions that multiply to give

(a) $4x^3y^2$ (b) $15x^3y^2$ (c) $12x^3$

(d) $16x^2y$ (e) $3x^5y^2$ (f) $5x^4y^2$

8 Multiply out the brackets in each of these and simplify where possible.

(a) $3(2p - q) + 5(p + q)$ (b) $x(2x + xy) - 5x^2(x - y)$

9 Expand and simplify the following.

(a) $(4ab)^2$ (b) $(2mn)^3$ (c) $(4a^2b^3)^3$ (d) $\left(\dfrac{2p}{3rs^2}\right)^3$

10 Simplify each of these.

(a) $\dfrac{12x^2y}{3xy}$ (b) $\dfrac{9x^2y^3}{3x^2y^2}$ (c) $\dfrac{ab^2}{3b}$ (d) $\dfrac{4xy}{y^3}$

(e) $\dfrac{12k^2l^3m}{36klm}$ (f) $\dfrac{4ab \times 3a^2b}{6b}$ (g) $\dfrac{7mn^2 \times 3m^3n}{2mn^2}$ (h) $\dfrac{4a^2b^3 \times 2b^4}{3a^3b}$

11 Simplify each of these.

(a) $\dfrac{a^2b + 4ab}{ab}$ (b) $\dfrac{4xy^2 + x^2y^3}{xy^2}$ (c) $\dfrac{3h^2k^2 + 18h^2}{6h^2k}$ (d) $\dfrac{c^2d^2 + 5c^3d}{c^3d^3}$

E Expanding and factorising expressions

1 Expand each of these.

(a) $4(3a + 2b)$ (b) $b(4a - 5b)$ (c) $5(2a + 3b)$ (d) $x(y + x^2)$

2 Factorise each of these.

(a) $5a - 5b$ (b) $4a + 12b$ (c) $6n - 15m$ (d) $xy + 2x$

(e) $n^2 - 5nm$ (f) $ab + a^2$ (g) $3ab^2 - 7b$ (h) $a - 7a^4b$

3 Expand each of these.

(a) $ab(3a - 2b)$ (b) $6x(y + 3x)$ (c) $3k^2(4l + 5)$

4 Factorise each of these completely.

(a) $5mn^2 - 15m^2n$ (b) $x^2y + 3xy^3$ (c) $6k^2l^2 - 4kl$

(d) $3ab^2 + 6ab^3$ (e) $4p^2q^3 + 10p^3q$ (f) $5x^2y + 10y^3$

(g) $4x^2y^3 + 12x^4y^2$ (h) $16x^2y^3 - 4xy$ (i) $5x^4y + x^2y^3$

5

C	A	E	I	O	L	N	P	R	S	Y
3	$4x$	$3x$	xy	$3y^2$	$2x - y$	$xy - 1$	$3x + 2y$	$x^2y + 2$	$x + y$	$2x - 5y$

Fully factorise each expression below as the product of two factors.
Use the code above to find a letter for each factor.
Rearrange each set of letters to spell an item found in a school bag.

(a) $3x^2y + 2xy^2$, $3x^2y - 3x$, $6x - 3y$

(b) $6xy^2 - 15y^3$, $3x^2y + 6$, $4x^2y - 4x$

(c) $4x^3y + 8x$, $3x^2 + 3xy$, $3x^3y + 6x$

F Finding and simplifying formulas

1 **(a)** Find a formula for the perimeter of each shape below.
Use P to stand for the perimeter each time.

(b) Find a formula for the area of each shape.
Use A to stand for the area each time.

(i)

$3x$
$4y$

(ii)
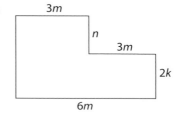
$3m$
n
$3m$
$2k$
$6m$

2 **(a)** Find a formula for the volume (V) of each prism.

(b) Find a formula for the surface area (S) of each prism.

(i)
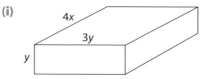
$4x$
$3y$
y

(ii)
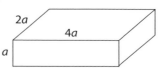
$2a$
$4a$
a

*3 **(a)** Find a formula for the volume of each prism.

(b) Find a formula for the surface area of each prism.

(i)
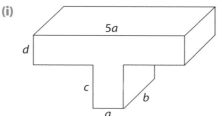
$5a$
d
c
b
a

(ii)
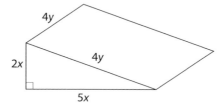
$4y$
$4y$
$2x$
$5x$

16 Coordinates in three dimensions

A Identifying points

1 A cuboid is positioned on a 3-D grid as shown.
It has vertices at (3, 0, 0), (0, 1, 0) and (0, 0, 2).

Write down the coordinates of the other five vertices.

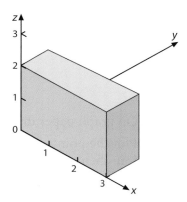

2 This shape is made from five cubes.

(a) What is the letter for the point (3, 1, 1)?

(b) Write down the coordinates of the
other five labelled points.

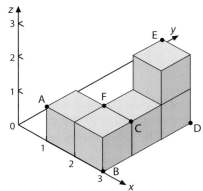

3 This T-shape is made from five cubes.
Point P is at (1, 1, 1).

Give the coordinates of the other four labelled points.

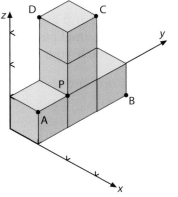

4 A cuboid is positioned on a 3-D centimetre grid with vertices at
(1, 1, 1), (3, 1, 1), (1, 1, 3) and (3, 4, 1).

(a) Write down the coordinates of the other four vertices.

(b) What is the volume of the cuboid?

17 Cubic graphs and equations

1 (a) Copy and complete this table of values for $y = x^3 - 5x$.

x	⁻3	⁻2.5	⁻2	⁻1.5	⁻1	⁻0.5	0	0.5	1	1.5	2	2.5	3
$y = x^3 - 5x$													

(b) On graph paper draw axes as shown.

Plot the points from your table.
Join them up with a smooth curve
to show the graph of $y = x^3 - 5x$.

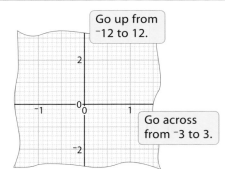

Go up from
⁻12 to 12.

Go across
from ⁻3 to 3.

(c) Describe any symmetry the graph has.

(d) From the graph, estimate the values of x
for which $x^3 - 5x = 3$, correct to 1 d.p.

(e) Use the graph to show that the equation
$x^3 - 5x = 8$ has only one solution.

2 Helen is using trial and improvement to find
a solution to the equation $x^3 + 2x = 20$.
The table shows her first two trials.

Copy and continue the table to find
a solution to the equation.
Give your answer correct to 1 d.p.

x	$x^3 + 2x$	Comment
2	12	Too small
3	33	Too big

3 Use a trial and improvement method to find the value of x correct
to one decimal place when $x^3 + 8x = 120$.
Show clearly your trials and their outcomes.

4 (a) Copy and complete this table of values for $y = x^3 - 3x + 1$.

x	⁻2	⁻1.5	⁻1	⁻0.5	0	0.5	1	1.5	2
$y = x^3 - 3x + 1$	⁻1								

(b) On graph paper draw axes with x from ⁻2 to 2 and y from ⁻2 to 4.
Draw the graph of $y = x^3 - 3x + 1$.

(c) (i) Show that the equation $x^3 - 3x + 1 = 0$ has a solution between 1.5 and 2.

(ii) Use trial and improvement to find that solution, correct to 2 d.p.
Show clearly your trials and their outcomes.

18 Gradients and rates

A Gradient of a sloping line

1 Find the gradient of each of these lines.

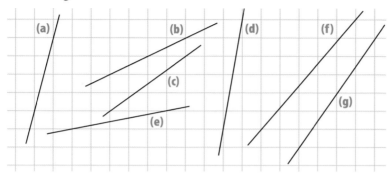

2 Find the gradient of the line joining the points with coordinates (2, 3) and (7, 7).

3 In Wengen, Switzerland, a cable car takes you up to the nearest peak.
The cable car starts at a height of 1300 m above sea level.
The peak is at a height of 2229 m above sea level.

According to the map, the horizontal distance covered is 1280 m.

(a) What height does the cable car climb?

(b) What is the average gradient of the climb, correct to three decimal places?

B Positive and negative gradients

1 Find the gradient of each of these lines.

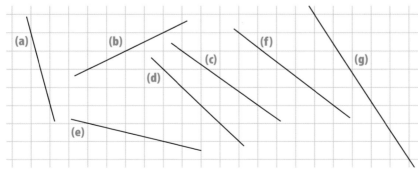

2 Find the gradients of the lines joining

  (a) (6, 5) and (1, 3)   **(b)** (0, 4) and (4, 0)   **(c)** ($^-$1, $^-$4) and (2, 5)

  (d) ($^-$2, 0) and (2, $^-$8)   **(e)** (5, $^-$2) and (1, 4)   **(f)** ($^-$3, $^-$1) and (2, $^-$4)

c Interpreting a gradient as a rate

1 (a) Work out the gradient of each line below.

(b) What does each gradient represent?

(i)

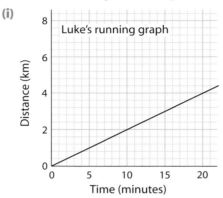

(ii)

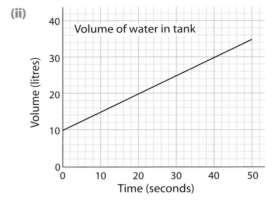

2 (a) Work out the gradient of this line, correct to 1 d.p.

(b) What does the gradient represent?

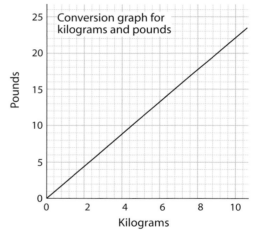

3 The graph shows the temperature experienced as a mountaineer climbs up a mountain.

(a) Calculate the gradient of the line.

(b) What does the gradient represent?

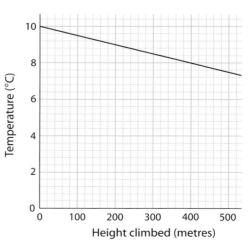

4 Roger walks from Vendrell to the beach at Salvador and then returns to Vendrell.
The travel graph of his journey is shown.
Describe each stage of the journey, giving times taken and speeds.

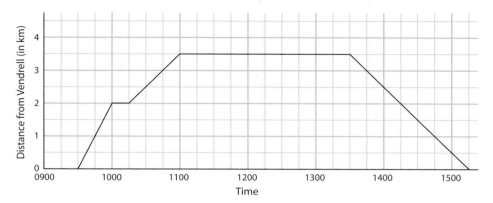

D Calculating with rates

1 Rohini earns £34.10 for $5\frac{1}{2}$ hours' work. What is her hourly rate of pay?

2 Matthew's typing speed is 65 words per minute.
How many hours, to the nearest half hour, will it take him to type
a 25 000 word thesis?

3 A researcher finds that, when hovering, a hummingbird completes
100 wingbeats in 1.3 seconds.
What rate is this, in wingbeats per second?

4 (a) A cog in a machine rotates once in 7.5 seconds.
At what speed is it rotating in revolutions per minute?

(b) Another cog rotates at the rate of 0.8 revolutions per second.
How long will it take to complete 1000 revolutions?

5 The world record for the number of stamps licked and stuck on to envelopes
in 5 minutes is 225.

What rate is this   (a) in stamps per second   (b) in seconds per stamp

6 Meg needs to print a 75-page document.
Her printer will print 15 pages per minute in draft quality or
9 pages per minute in best quality.
How much quicker will it be to print the document in draft rather than best quality?

*7 A small pump can empty a pool in 20 minutes working at 450 litres per minute.
A large pump could empty the same pool in 12 minutes.
How long would it take to empty the pool if both pumps worked together?

19 Changing the subject

1 Rearrange each of these formulas to make the bold letter the subject.

   (a) $k = 10\mathbf{h}$

   (b) $y = 3\mathbf{x} - 19$

   (c) $y = \dfrac{\mathbf{z} + 6}{5}$

   (d) $a = \dfrac{\mathbf{b} - 9}{11}$

   (e) $u = \dfrac{1 + \mathbf{v}}{5}$

   (f) $p = 15 + 2\mathbf{q}$

   (g) $h = \dfrac{2\mathbf{k} + 3}{7}$

   (h) $b = \dfrac{8\mathbf{c} - 5}{3}$

   (i) $j = \dfrac{13 + 9\mathbf{k}}{4}$

2 Rearrange each of these formulas to make x the subject.

   (a) $y = 7(x - 5)$

   (b) $y = 5(3 + 4x)$

   (c) $y = 2(3x - 1)$

3 Rearrange each of these formulas to make the bold letter the subject.

   (a) $g = \dfrac{\mathbf{h}}{2} + 3$

   (b) $f = \tfrac{1}{3}\mathbf{g} - 1$

   (c) $c = \dfrac{7\mathbf{d}}{2} - 4$

4 Rearrange each of these formulas to make the bold letter the subject.

   (a) $y = \dfrac{\mathbf{x} - 2}{7}$

   (b) $P = 9 + 5\mathbf{Q}$

   (c) $h = \dfrac{2\mathbf{k} - 7}{3}$

   (d) $z = \dfrac{\mathbf{y}}{4} + 1$

   (e) $A = 5(3\mathbf{B} - 2)$

   (f) $w = \dfrac{3\mathbf{v}}{10} + 5$

5 Rearrange each of these formulas to make the bold letter the subject.

   (a) $y + \mathbf{x} = 7$

   (b) $2\mathbf{G} - 5H = 9$

   (c) $h - \mathbf{k} = 3$

   (d) $a = 1 - \dfrac{\mathbf{b}}{3}$

   (e) $y = 7 - 5\mathbf{x}$

   (f) $p = 3(10 - \mathbf{q})$

   (g) $t = 4(2 - 5\mathbf{s})$

   (h) $b = \dfrac{2 - 5\mathbf{c}}{3}$

   (i) $J = 2 - \dfrac{7\mathbf{K}}{3}$

6 The equation of a graph is $y = 2x - 8$.

   (a) What is the value of y when $x = 5$?

   (b) Where does the graph cut the y-axis?

   (c) Rearrange the formula to make x the subject.

   (d) What is the value of x when $y = 6$?

   (e) Where does the graph cut the x-axis?

7 The equation of a graph is $y = \dfrac{3x + 1}{2}$.

    (a) Where does the graph cut the y-axis?

    (b) Rearrange the formula to make x the subject.

    (c) Where does the graph cut the x-axis?

C Formulas connecting more than two letters

1 Which of these are correct arrangements of $a = b - c$?

    P $\;b = a + c$ **Q** $\;b = c + a$ **R** $\;c = b - a$ **S** $\;c = a - b$

2 Rearrange each of these to make the bold letter the subject.

    (a) $r = s\boldsymbol{t}$ **(b)** $d = e + \boldsymbol{f}$ **(c)** $g = \boldsymbol{h} - p$ **(d)** $b = \dfrac{\boldsymbol{d}}{c}$

3 Rearrange each of these to make the bold letter the subject.

    (a) $h = 4\boldsymbol{k} + g$ **(b)** $y = z\boldsymbol{x} - 5$ **(c)** $w = a\boldsymbol{b} + 5c$ **(d)** $p = q(\boldsymbol{r} + 1)$

    (e) $h = \dfrac{g}{\boldsymbol{k}} + 9$ **(f)** $y = \dfrac{x + 3\boldsymbol{z}}{2}$ **(g)** $p = \dfrac{2(\boldsymbol{n} + 1)}{m}$ **(h)** $a = 4b + \dfrac{\boldsymbol{c}}{d}$

    (i) $y - \boldsymbol{x} = v$ **(j)** $P = Q - S\boldsymbol{T}$ **(k)** $m = 5n - \dfrac{7\boldsymbol{h}}{g}$ **(l)** $W = \dfrac{6(X - \boldsymbol{Y})}{Z}$

4 You are given that $r = mx - ny$.

    (a) Rearrange the formula to give y in terms of m, x, r and n.

    (b) Use your new formula to find y when $r = 22$, $m = 5$, $x = 2$ and $n = 4$.

5 A household gas bill is calculated using the formula

    $C = sd + nu$

C is the total cost in pence;
s is the standing charge in pence per day;
d is the number of days;
n is the number of units of gas used;
u is the cost of gas in pence per unit.

    (a) Rearrange the formula to give n in terms of the other variables.

    (b) For one customer, the standing charge is 10p per day and the cost per unit is 1.1p.

        (i) One of her bills is £80.94 for a period of 90 days.
            How many units of gas have been charged for?

        (ii) The cost for this customer's gas goes up.
            The standing charge stays the same.
            A new bill is £90.64 for 6280 units over a period of 90 days.

            What is the new cost of the gas in pence per unit?

D Squares and square roots

1 In each of these formulas x is a length and A is an area.
Make x the subject of each of these formulas.

(a) $A = 3x^2$ (b) $A = \dfrac{x^2}{5}$ (c) $A = x^2 - 2$ (d) $A = \dfrac{x^2}{7} + 9$

2 A cuboid has a square cross-section
with edges of length x.
The length of the cuboid is $3x$.

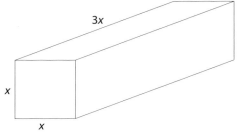

(a) Show that its total surface area is
given by the formula $A = 14x^2$.

(b) Make x the subject of the formula.

(c) Find the dimensions of one of these cuboids with a total surface area of $100\,\text{cm}^2$.
(Give your answer to the nearest $0.1\,\text{cm}$.)

3 Each of these is the equation of a graph where x can take any value.
Make x the subject of each one.

(a) $y = x^2 + 7$ (b) $y = 7x^2 + 5$ (c) $y = \dfrac{x^2}{7} - 3$ (d) $y = (x + 7)^2$

4 The equation of a graph is $y = 18x^2 - 2$.

(a) Find the value of y when $x = 0$.

(b) Make x the subject of the equation.

(c) What are the coordinates of the points where the graph intersects the x-axis?

5 A cuboid has a square cross-section with edges of length b.
The length of the cuboid is a.

(a) Find a formula for the volume V of the cuboid.

(b) Make b the subject of the formula.

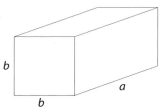

6 Make x the subject of each formula.

(a) $y = \sqrt{x} + 5$ (b) $y = \sqrt{x-5}$ (c) $y = \sqrt{5x}$ (d) $y = \sqrt{5x+1}$

(e) $y = \sqrt{5x} + 1$ (f) $y = \sqrt{\dfrac{x}{5}}$ (g) $y = \sqrt{x-z}$ (h) $y = \sqrt{\dfrac{x}{z}} - 7$

20 Probability

A Relative frequency

1   Marco has a tetrahedral dice.
    He throws it 40 times and records the number that lands face down each time.

2	1	2	4	3	1	3	4	2	1
2	4	4	3	2	1	2	3	4	2
1	3	2	3	4	1	2	3	2	1
4	1	3	4	2	4	3	1	2	1

    (a) Find the relative frequency of each score after 40 throws.

    (b) Comment on the fairness of Marco's dice.

    (c) Estimate the number of times a 2 will occur in   (i)   100 throws   (ii)   1000 throws

2   Mark catches the train to work every day.
    He keeps a record of the train's punctuality.

Punctuality	early	on time	less than 10 minutes late	between 10 and 30 minutes late	30 minutes or more late
Frequency	8	91	110	28	13

    (a) Estimate the probability that the train is early or on time.

    (b) Mark gets compensation if the train is 30 minutes or more late.
         Estimate the probability that he gets compensation.

3   A sample of cars of a certain model are tested for engine and brake faults
    one year after manufacture.
    The results are summarised in this table.

Description	Number of cars
No engine or brake fault	22
Engine fault but no brake fault	19
Brake fault but no engine fault	31
Both brake and engine faults	18

    (a) Estimate the probability that one of these cars chosen at random has

         (i)   no engine or brake fault

         (ii) an engine fault (with or without a brake fault)

         (iii) a brake fault

    (b) If 1000 of this model are tested one year after manufacture, how many
         would you expect to have both brake and engine faults?

B Equally likely outcomes

1 Two bags, A and B, contain coloured sweets.
Bag A contains 3 red and 5 green sweets.
Bag B contains 3 red and 9 yellow sweets.

  (a) A sweet is picked at random from bag A.
  What is the probability that it is red?

  (b) The contents of the two bags are poured into an empty bag.
  A sweet is picked at random from this bag.
  What is the probability that the sweet is   **(i)** red   **(ii)** not red   **(iii)** yellow

2 Laura has a set of cards numbered from 1 to 20.
She picks out one card at random.

  What is the probability that she picks a card that is

  (a) a square number   **(b)** a multiple of 3

  (c) a factor of 12   **(d)** a prime number

  (e) **not** a multiple of 5   **(f)** **not** a triangle number

3 These are the results of a class survey.

	Boys	Girls
Left-handed	1	3
Right-handed	11	13

  (a) A boy in the class is chosen at random.
  What is the probability that he is right-handed?

  (b) A pupil is chosen at random from the class.
  What is the probability that the pupil is left-handed?

  (c) A left-handed child is chosen from the class.
  What is the probability that this child is a girl?

4 Daniel has a pack of eight cards. They look the same on one side,
but are coloured red, blue or green on the other side.

  A friend picks a card at random and notes its colour. The card is then
  replaced and the pack shuffled. This process is repeated again and again.

  Here are the results of 80 trials.

Colour	Red	Blue	Green
Frequency	19	52	9

  How many cards of each colour do you think are in the pack?

c Listing outcomes

1 Roffey Robins need to choose a new football strip consisting of a top and shorts.
They can choose from a black, white or striped top and black or white shorts.

    (a) Make a list of all the possible combinations of strips that could be chosen.

    (b) If a top and a pair of shorts are chosen at random, what is
the probability they are both black or both white?

2 Two people from this group are chosen at random for a beach volleyball team.

    Alan   Bob   Cara   Dave   Ella

    (a) Make a list of all the possible pairs for the team.

    (b) What is the probability that Dave gets chosen for the team?

    (c) What is the probability that the pair chosen will be

        (i) both female   **(ii)** both male

3 These two spinners are fair.
Aisha spins them both together.

 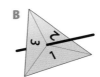

    (a) Copy the table and show all
the possible results and the total scores.

Spinner A	Spinner B	Total score

    (b) What is the probability that Aisha will get a total score of 4 or more?

4 When an ordinary dice is rolled, the score can be either even or odd
and these two outcomes are equally likely.

    A dice is rolled four times.

    (a) Copy and complete this list of all the possible arrangements of
odd and even scores (E = even, O = odd):

        EEEE, EEEO, …

    (b) Find the probability that

        (i) there are more even than odd scores

        (ii) there are the same number of odd and even scores

        (iii) the total of the four scores is odd

D Showing outcomes on a grid

1 Alastair has a fair spinner with seven equal sectors.
He spins it twice and adds the scores together.

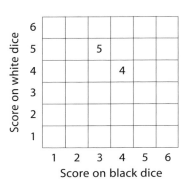

(a) Use a grid to list all the possible outcomes.

(b) What is the most likely total score for the two spins?

(c) What is the probability that Alastair scores

(i) a number greater than 7   (ii) a multiple of 3

2 Marsha has two ordinary dice, one black and one white.
She rolls them and notes the higher of the two scores.
(If they are equal, she notes that score.)

(a) Copy and complete the grid, to show all the
possible outcomes.

(b) Find the probability that the higher of the two
scores is

(i) 3   (ii) less than 3   (iii) greater than 4

3 A spinner has six equal sectors numbered 1, 2, 2, 3, 3, 3.
The spinner is spun twice and the two scores are added.

(a) Copy and complete this grid to show all the possible outcomes.

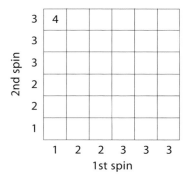

(b) Find the probability that the total of the two scores is

(i) 4   (ii) 5 or 6   (iii) less than 3

4 Julie has two spinners.
Spinner A has four equal sectors numbered 1, 2, 3, 4.
Spinner B has five equal sectors numbered 1, 2, 3, 4, 5.

Julie spins them both.
Find the probability that the total score is greater than 4.

Mixed practice 3

You need graph paper.

1. A set of twenty cards have the numbers 1 to 20 marked on them.
   What is the probability that the number on a randomly picked card is prime?

2. Expand these.

   (a) $7(p - q)$ **(b)** $4(a + 3c)$ **(c)** $p(p - 3q)$ **(d)** $5xy(3x - 4)$

3. The cuboid has vertices at $(0, 0, 0)$, $(0, 3, 4)$ and $(5, 0, 0)$ as shown.

   Write down the coordinates of the vertices labelled A, B, C and D.

   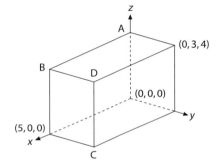

4. Find the value of $\frac{1}{2}p(q - 3)$ when $p = {}^-3$ and $q = 1$.

5. Northside Bus Company keep a record of any delays on their buses.

   Out of 500 journeys, 123 buses were on time, 272 were less than 10 minutes late and the rest were more than 10 minutes late.
   Estimate the probability that a bus will be more than 10 minutes late.

6. **(a)** Show that the area of triangle PQR is given by $A = 8x^2$.

   (b) Rearrange the formula to make x the subject.

   (c) Find the value of x if the triangle has area $200\,\text{cm}^2$.

   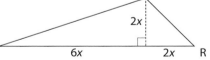

7. The equation $x^3 + 2x = 24$ has a solution between 2 and 3.
   Use trial and improvement to find this solution.
   Show all your trials and give your answer correct to one decimal place.

8. Simplify each of these.

   (a) $n^2 + 5n + 2n^2 - 7n$ **(b)** $\dfrac{n^2 - 6n}{n}$ **(c)** $\dfrac{ab^2 + 2a^2b}{ab}$

9. A hosepipe delivers water at the rate of 540 litres per hour.
   How many litres does it deliver in half a minute?

10. Rearrange each of these formulas to make the bold letter the subject.

    (a) $b = 4(\boldsymbol{a} - 1)$ **(b)** $q = \dfrac{3\boldsymbol{p} - 1}{2}$ **(c)** $d = 5 - 3\boldsymbol{c}$ **(d)** $t = 8 + \dfrac{\boldsymbol{s}}{2}$

11 Find the gradient of the straight line that joins points $(4, 2)$ and $(10, 7)$, correct to 2 d.p.

12 Simplify these expressions.

    (a) $5x \times 2y \times 3z$ **(b)** $6a^2b^3 \times 4ab^2$ **(c)** $\dfrac{f^8 \times fg^5}{g^4}$ **(d)** $\dfrac{6p^6r \times 2pq}{4p^2q^5}$

13 Azmat has a spinner with three sections – red, yellow, blue.
The probability that it shows red is 0.26.
The probability that it shows yellow is 0.35.

    (a) What is the probability that it shows blue?

    (b) Azmat spins the spinner 400 times.
        Estimate the number of times it will show yellow.

14 Factorise these expressions completely.

    (a) $5x^2 - 5xy$ **(b)** $8ab^2 + 2$ **(c)** $9y^3 - 12x^2y$ **(d)** $6p^2q + 10pq^2$

15 The fuel consumption of a van is 13.6 litres per 100 km.
Calculate the distance that the van can travel on 66 litres of fuel.

16 Rearrange each of these formulas to make the bold letter the subject.

    (a) $y = \sqrt{\boldsymbol{x}} + z$ **(b)** $y = ax - 3\boldsymbol{b}$ **(c)** $w = \dfrac{\boldsymbol{u} - st}{n}$ **(d)** $t = \dfrac{p + \boldsymbol{q}^2}{r}$

17 Suzie has two fair spinners, numbered as shown.
She spins them and finds the total of the two scores.

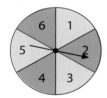  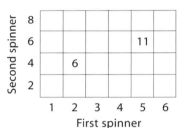

    (a) Copy and complete the grid showing all the possible outcomes of the two spins.

    (b) Find the probability that the total of the two scores is

        (i) 9   **(ii)** less than 8   **(iii)** greater than 10

18 (a) Copy and complete this table
       of values of $y = x^3 - 4x - 2$.

x	-3	-2	-1	0	1	2	3
y	-17			1			

    (b) On graph paper, draw axes with x from -3 to 3 and y from -20 to 20.
        Draw the graph of $y = x^3 - 4x - 2$.

    (c) **(i)** Show that $x^3 - 4x - 2 = 0$ has a solution between 2 and 3.

        (ii) Use your graph to estimate this solution, correct to 1 d.p.

21 Large and small numbers

A Powers of ten

1 Write these numbers as powers of ten.

   (a) $10 \times 10 \times 10 \times 10$ **(b)** 1000

   (c) 100 000   **(d)** ten million

2 Put these numbers in order of size, starting with the smallest.

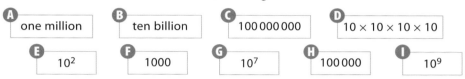

Ⓐ one million   **Ⓑ** ten billion   **Ⓒ** 100 000 000   **Ⓓ** $10 \times 10 \times 10 \times 10$

Ⓔ 10^2 **Ⓕ** 1000   **Ⓖ** 10^7 **Ⓗ** 100 000   **Ⓘ** 10^9

3 Write these as single powers of ten.

   (a) $10^5 \times 10^6$ **(b)** $10^3 \times 10 \times 10^2$ **(c)** $\dfrac{10^5}{10^2}$ **(d)** $\dfrac{10^2 \times 10^4}{10^3}$

4 Evaluate these.

   (a) $17 \times 100\,000$ **(b)** 5.26×10^4 **(c)** $61.9 \times 10\,000$ **(d)** 72.3×10^5

B Writing large numbers in different ways

1 Write the numbers in these sentences in figures.

   (a) The remotest object visible without the aid of a telescope is 2.3 million light-years away.

   (b) The Sun will stop shining in about 5 billion years.

   (c) The surface area of the Earth is more than 510 million square kilometres.

   (d) The Moon is about 380 thousand kilometres from the Earth.

   (e) The brightest star in the sky has a diameter of 2.33 million kilometres.

2 The table shows the areas of the seven largest oceans and seas.

   (a) Copy the table, writing the areas in millions to the nearest million km^2.

   (b) The total area of sea is about 360 million km^2.
       What percentage of the sea is taken up by the Pacific Ocean?

Pacific Ocean	155 557 000 km²
Atlantic Ocean	76 762 000 km²
Indian Ocean	68 556 000 km²
Southern Ocean	20 327 000 km²
Arctic Ocean	14 056 000 km²
South China Sea	2 975 000 km²
Carribean Sea	2 516 000 km²

C Standard form for large numbers

1 Write these numbers in standard form.

   (a) 4 000 000   (b) 28 000   (c) 603 000   (d) 32 000 000 000

2 Write these numbers in ordinary form.

   (a) 3×10^5 (b) 1×10^8 (c) 6.3×10^3 (d) 2.86×10^7

3 (a) The table shows the amounts of different materials collected for recycling and composting by local authorities in England in 2003/04.

   Rewrite the table, giving the amounts in standard form.

Material	Amount (tonnes)
Paper and card	1 271 000
Glass	568 000
Garden waste	1 360 000
Cans	43 000
Plastic	17 000

   (b) The total amount collected for recycling and composting in England in 2003/04 was 4.52 million tonnes.
   Write this number in standard form.

4 The circumference of the Earth is approximately 4×10^7 m.
   Write this distance as an ordinary number.

5 The average distance of the Sun from the Earth is 1.49×10^8 km.
   Write this in ordinary form.

D Using a calculator for large numbers in standard form

1 The values of r, s, t and u are

   $$r = 5\,000\,000 \qquad s = 80\,000 \qquad t = 40\,000\,000 \qquad u = 0.002$$

   Evaluate each expression below and give your answer in standard form.

   (a) rs (b) s^2 (c) rtu (d) $\dfrac{t}{u}$ (e) $r^2 + s^2$

2 Write the answer to each of these calculations in standard form, correct to three significant figures.

   (a) $42\,360 \times 5\,300\,000$ (b) $343\,000^2 + 417\,000^2$ (c) $\dfrac{49\,000}{0.004\,07}$

3 Give the answer to each of these calculations in standard form, correct to two significant figures.

   (a) $(8.62 \times 10^8) + (1.4 \times 10^9)$ (b) $(2.49 \times 10^6) \times (4.13 \times 10^8)$

   (c) $\dfrac{7.18 \times 10^{15}}{4.1 \times 10^3}$ (d) $\sqrt{\dfrac{2.3 \times 10^{20}}{4.9 \times 10^8}}$

4 The table shows the population (in 2006) and the area of some countries.

Country	Population	Area (km²)
Brazil	1.9×10^8	8.5×10^6
China	1.3×10^9	9.6×10^6
India	1.1×10^9	3.3×10^6
Russia	1.4×10^8	1.7×10^7
South Africa	4.4×10^7	1.2×10^6
United Kingdom	6.0×10^7	2.4×10^5
United States	3.0×10^8	9.6×10^6

(a) Calculate the population density of each of the seven countries, giving your answers correct to one significant figure.

(b) Write the countries in order of population density, highest first.

E Standard form for small numbers

1 Write these numbers in ordinary form.

(a) 1×10^{-2} (b) 2.3×10^{-4} (c) 3.8×10^{-6} (d) 8.08×10^{-7}

2 Write these numbers in standard form.

(a) $0.000\,003$ (b) $0.000\,006\,72$ (c) $0.000\,300\,8$ (d) $0.000\,000\,000\,004$

3 If you take four cards from a pack of playing cards, the probability that they are all aces is $0.000\,003\,69$ (correct to 3 s.f.).

(a) Which of these are ways of writing this probability?

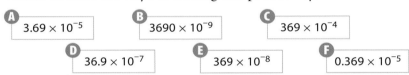

(b) Write the probability in standard form.

4 The probability of rolling six consecutive sixes when rolling a standard dice six times is 2.14×10^{-5} (correct to 3 s.f.).
Write this probability in ordinary form.

F Using a calculator for small numbers in standard form

1 Write the answer to each of these calculations in standard form, correct to three significant figures.

(a) $(3.8 \times 10^{-4}) \times (4.1 \times 10^{-1})$ (b) $(8.72 \times 10^{-4})^2$

(c) $\dfrac{4.6 \times 10^{-8}}{7.2 \times 10^5}$ (d) $\sqrt{\dfrac{6.39 \times 10^7}{4.07 \times 10^{-3}}}$

2 Given that $x = 3.5 \times 10^{-6}$ and $y = 9.05 \times 10^{-5}$, calculate the values of these expressions, giving your answers in standard form correct to three significant figures.

(a) $x + y$ (b) xy (c) $x^2 y$ (d) $x \div y$

3 Calculate the area of a circular ink dot which has a diameter of 3.6×10^{-2} cm.

4 The mass of an atom is measured in amus (atomic mass units).
An amu is $1.660\,33 \times 10^{-27}$ kg.

(a) The mass of an atom of lead is 207.19 amus.
In kilograms, this is $207.19 \times (1.660\,33 \times 10^{-27})$.
Find the mass of one atom of lead, in kg, in standard form correct to 3 s.f.

(b) The mass of an atom of copper is 63.546 amus.
Work out the mass of one atom of copper, in kg, in standard form correct to 3 s.f.

(c) The mass of an atom of zinc is 65.381 amus.
How much more, in kg, is the mass of one atom of zinc than one atom of copper?

G Standard form without a calculator

1 Given that $a = 4 \times 10^3$ and $b = 5 \times 10^4$, calculate these,
giving each answer in standard form.

(a) $3a$ (b) $2b$ (c) $b - a$ (d) ab (e) $a \div b$

2 Calculate these, giving your answers in standard form.

(a) $(4 \times 10^6) \times (5 \times 10^3)$ (b) $(8 \times 10^5) + (3 \times 10^6)$

(c) $(5 \times 10^3)^2$ (d) $\dfrac{6 \times 10^{-5}}{1.2 \times 10^3}$

3 Calculate these, giving your answers in ordinary form.

(a) $(3 \times 10^3) \times 10^5$ (b) $(2 \times 10^4) - (5 \times 10^3)$ (c) $(7 \times 10^{-9}) \times (1.5 \times 10^4)$

(d) $\dfrac{3.6 \times 10^3}{10^5}$ (e) $\dfrac{4.8 \times 10^4}{1.2 \times 10^{-2}}$ (f) $(3.2 \times 10^5) + (6.4 \times 10^4)$

4 Blood contains about 5×10^6 red blood corpuscles per mm³.

(a) How many red blood corpuscles will there be in a 4 mm³ drop of blood?

(b) The average adult has about 5×10^6 mm³ of blood in their body.
How many red blood corpuscles will there be in the average adult's body?

5 (a) Round each of these numbers to one significant figure.

| $A = 2.362 \times 10^8$ | $B = 2.886 \times 10^{-7}$ | $C = 4.724 \times 10^{-3}$ | $D = 6.448 \times 10^{10}$ |

(b) Use your answers to work out an estimate for each of these calculations.
Give each estimate in standard form.

(i) $A \times B$ (ii) $B \times D$ (iii) $B \times C$

(iv) $D \div A$ (v) $B \div D$ (vi) $C \div A$

22 The tangent function

A Finding an opposite side

1 Find the opposite side in each of these right-angled triangles.
Give your answers correct to one decimal place.

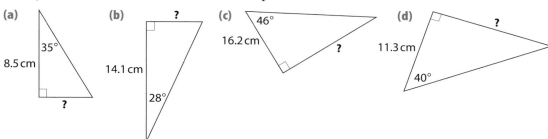

B Finding an adjacent side

1 Find the adjacent side in each of these right-angled triangles,
giving your answers to 1 d.p.

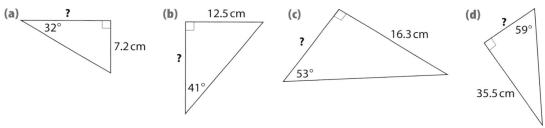

2 Find the missing sides, to 1 d.p. Some are opposite and some are adjacent.

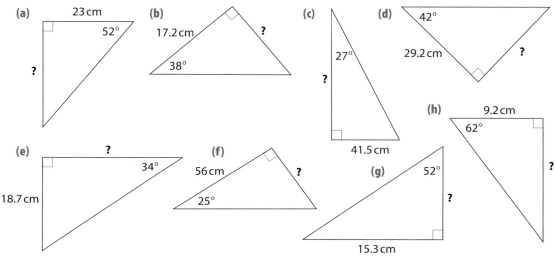

C Finding an angle

1 Find the angle marked with a letter in each of these triangles, to the nearest 0.1°.

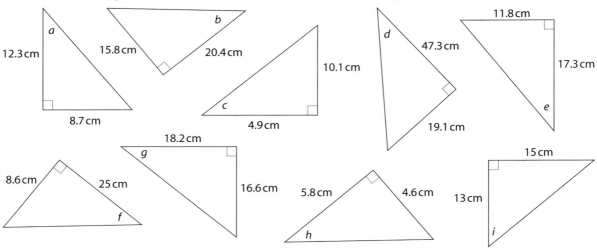

D Mixed questions

1 Find each length or angle marked with a **?**, giving answers to 1 d.p.

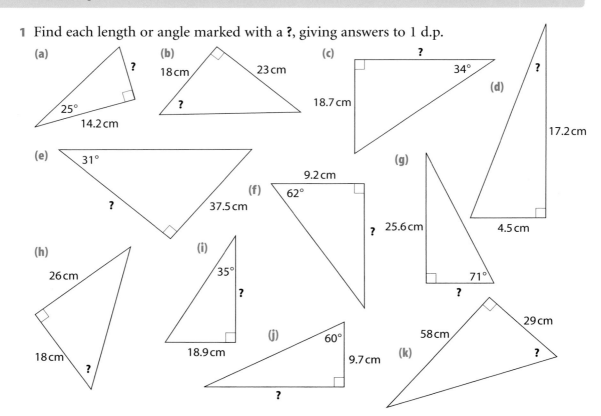

2 The diagram shows the end view of a ridge tent.
Calculate the length of the base.

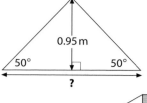

3 A tower is 21 m high.
Point R is 45 m from the base of the tower.

Calculate the angle of elevation
of the top of the tower from R.

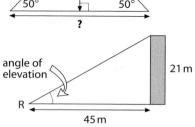

4 Zara starts from A, walks 9 km east to B
and then walks 4 km south to C.
Find the bearing of C from A.

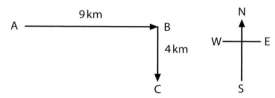

5 The coordinates of the vertices of triangle PQR are P (2, 5), Q (6, 12) and R (6, 5).
Find angle RPQ.

6 XYZ is an isosceles triangle.
Find its area.

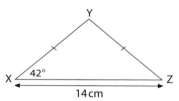

7 The acute angle between the diagonals in this rectangle is 50°.
The shorter side of the rectangle is 10 cm.
Find the length of the longer side.

8 Find the area of this rectangle.

9 In this kite angle BAD = 74°.
Find angle BCD.

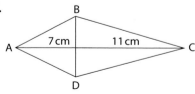

*10 Find the area of triangle PQR.

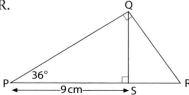

23 Linear equations 2

B Forming equations to solve word problems

1 There are three piles of stones.

Pile A has x stones.
Pile B has twice as many as pile A.
Pile C has 6 fewer than pile A.

(a) Write expressions in terms of x for the number of stones in pile B and pile C.

(b) Write an expression in terms of x for the total number of stones in the three piles.

(c) The total number of stones in the three piles is 94.
Form an equation and solve it to find the number of stones in pile A.

2 A pencil costs t pence.
A rubber costs 5 pence more than a pencil.
A sharpener costs 3 times as much as a pencil.

(a) Write expressions for

(i) the cost of six pencils

(ii) the cost of three rubbers

(b) The total cost of six pencils, three rubbers and a sharpener is 207 pence.

(i) Form an equation and solve it.

(ii) Find the cost of each item.

3 Xander and Zita each have the same number of pens.
Xander has three full boxes of pens and two loose pens.
Zita has two full boxes of pens and 14 loose pens.

Let b be the number of pens in a full box.

(a) Form an equation and solve it.

(b) How many pens does Zita have altogether?

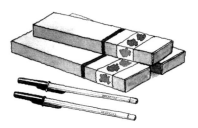

4 Greg is 7 years older than his cousin Eve.
In four years time, Greg will be twice as old as Eve.
Work out how old Greg and Eve are now.

c Mixed questions

1 Jake and Vicky both think of the same number.
Jake adds 1 and then multiplies by 6.
Vicky subtracts 3 and then multiplies by 3.
They both end up with the same answer.

What number were they both thinking of?

2 Find the size of each angle in this triangle.

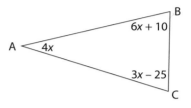

3 The perimeter of this rectangle is 120 cm.
Find the length of the longest side.

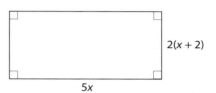

4 Three friends, Jade, Kyle and Sam, and a monkey are shipwrecked on an island with a crate of 185 bananas. They eat all the bananas.

Jade ate three more bananas than Sam.

Kyle ate eleven bananas fewer than Sam.

The monkey ate ten bananas.

Let n be the number of bananas that Sam ate.

Form an equation and solve it to find the number of bananas that Sam ate.

5 The area of this triangle is 40 cm². Form an equation in x and solve it.

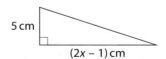

6 A linear sequence is 5, 8, 11, 14, 17, …

(a) Find an expression for the nth term of this sequence.

(b) One of the terms of this sequence is 500. Which term is it?

(c) Decide whether or not 700 is a term in this sequence.

24 Loci and constructions

You need a pair of compasses for all sections.

A The locus of points a fixed distance from a point or line

1 This is the plan view of a large machine in a factory.
   Draw the plan to scale.
   It is dangerous to be within 2 m of any part of this machine.
   Shade on your plan the danger zone around the machine.

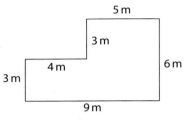

2 Mark two points Q and R, 7 cm apart.

   • Q   • R

   (a) Draw the locus of points that are 5 cm from Q.

   (b) Draw the locus of points that are 4 cm from R.

   (c) Shade the region where all the points are less than 5 cm from Q and
        more than 4 cm from R.

3 A target for a darts game is an equilateral triangle with a side length of 100 cm.

   (a) Make a scale diagram of this triangle using a scale of 1 cm to 10 cm.

   (b) If a dart lands inside the triangle and is not more than 20 cm from
        the sides of the triangle, it scores 10 points.
        Shade the area where you can score 10 points.

   (c) If a dart lands outside the triangle and is not more than 20 cm from
        the sides of the triangle, it scores 20 points. Otherwise, it scores nothing.
        Shade the area where you can score 20 points.

   (d) Label clearly the different score areas.

B The locus of points equidistant from two points
C The shortest route from a point to a line

1 Draw a large circle on plain paper and label the centre O.

   (a) Mark any two points P and Q on the circumference.
        Draw the locus of points equidistant from P and Q.

   (b) Mark another two points R and S on the circumference.
        Draw the locus of points equidistant from R and S.

   (c) What do you notice?

2 Draw a circle and mark three points A, B, C on it.

Construct the locus of all the points inside the circle that are nearer to A than to either B or C.

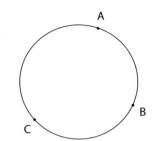

3 Construct accurately the triangle sketched here.

Show the following loci by shading, using only a ruler and compasses to find the boundaries.

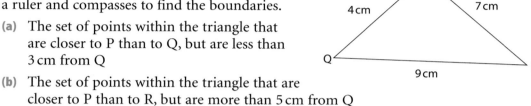

(a) The set of points within the triangle that are closer to P than to Q, but are less than 3 cm from Q

(b) The set of points within the triangle that are closer to P than to R, but are more than 5 cm from Q

4 Draw line segments AB, AC and AD like this. Lengths and angles do not have to be exactly as here.

Use a ruler and compasses only for the following.

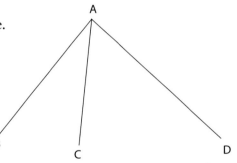

(a) Construct the perpendicular bisector of AC. Label O, the mid-point of AC.

(b) Construct a perpendicular from C to AB, meeting AB at P.

(c) Construct a perpendicular from C to AD, meeting AD at Q.

(d) Draw a circle, centre O, going through A and C. What do you notice?

5 Construct accurately the triangle sketched here.

(a) Using a ruler and compasses only, construct the line from A that is perpendicular to the side BC. Label the point D where this line meets BC.

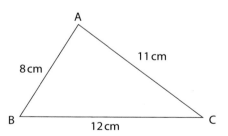

(b) Measure AD and use this length to calculate the area of the triangle.

(c) Explain why a perpendicular from C to AB should be 1.5 times as long as AD.

(d) Draw this perpendicular using a ruler and compasses only. Then measure to see whether you get the expected length.

D The locus of points equidistant from two lines

1 Draw this rectangle accurately.

Use only a ruler and compasses to find the lines required for the following loci.

A ── 8 cm ── B
6 cm
D ──────── C

(a) Show the set of points within the rectangle that are the same distance from line AD as from line AB.

(b) Show by shading the set of points in the rectangle that are closer to line AB than to line AD and less than 3 cm from C.

(c) Show by shading the set of points in the rectangle that are closer to AB than to BC and less than 5 cm from C.

2 Use a ruler and compasses only for the constructions needed in this question.

B
8 cm   4 cm
A   9 cm   C

(a) Construct this triangle accurately.

(b) Bisect angle BAC.

(c) Mark the point P that is equidistant from A and C and the same distance from lines AB and AC.

(d) Shade the region inside the triangle where all the points are nearer to AC than AB and less than 6 cm from C.

3 Use a ruler and compasses only to construct

(a) an angle of 120°   (b) an angle of $22\frac{1}{2}°$ (c) an angle of 105°

4 A quadrilateral has a point inside it that is equidistant from all four sides. Say whether the quadrilateral could be each of these, illustrating each answer with a sketch.

(a) A square   (b) A rectangle that is not a square

(c) A rhombus   (d) A parallelogram that is not a rhombus

(e) A kite that is not a rhombus (f) A trapezium that is not a rhombus

E The perpendicular from a point on a line

1 (a) Draw a line about 8 cm long and mark on it a point A.

(b) Mark a point B about 3 cm from the line.

(c) Use ruler and compasses only to construct the circle that passes through B and touches the line at A (so the line is a tangent to the circle).

Hint: What can you say about the distance from the centre of the circle to A and B?

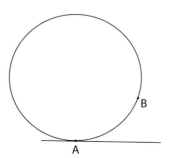

25 Equations of linear graphs

You need squared paper in section AB.

A Gradient and intercept of a linear graph
B Finding the equation of a graph

1 For each line below   **(i)**   state the gradient and y-intercept
                          (ii)   write down its equation

(a) 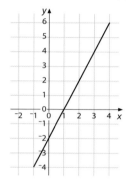   **(b)** 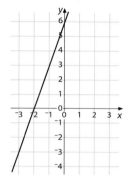   **(c)**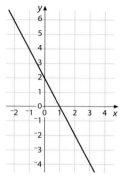

2 Write down the equation of the line with gradient $^-10$ that crosses the y-axis at $(0, 4)$.

3 Plot the points $(1, 9)$ and $(^-2, ^-3)$ on suitable axes.
Join the points and find the equation of the line.

4 For each line below   **(i)**   find the gradient and write it as a decimal
                          (ii)   find its equation

(a) 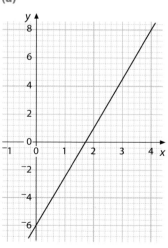   **(b)** 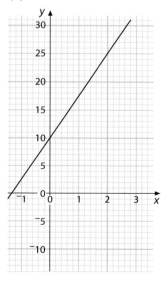   **(c)**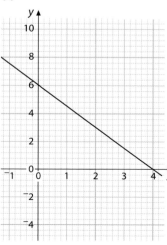

5 Write down the gradient and *y*-intercept of each of these lines.

(a) $y = 12x - 20$ (b) $y = x + 7$ (c) $y = {}^-6x - 1$

6 What is the equation of the line parallel to $y = 1.5x - 3$ that crosses the *y*-axis at $(0, 7)$?

7 Write down the equation of the line with *y*-intercept 5 that is parallel to $y = 3 - 9x$.

8 The lines labelled A to D match these equations.

P $y = 2x - 4$ **Q** $y = 2x + 4$

R $y = x - 4$ **S** $y = {}^-2x + 4$

Match each line to its correct equation.

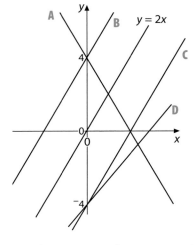

9 What is the equation of the line parallel to $y = 2x - 3$ that crosses the *y*-axis at $(0, 4)$?

10 Write down the equation of the line with *y*-intercept ${}^-5$ that is parallel to $y = 3 + 9x$.

11 (a) On a set of axes, draw the line with a gradient of ${}^-3$ that goes through $(2, {}^-2)$.

(b) What is the equation of this line?

c Equation of a line through two given points

1 Find, in the form $y = mx + c$, the equation of the line through

(a) $(0, 4)$ and $(1, 5)$ (b) $(0, 6)$ and $(6, 0)$

(c) $(4, 70)$ and $(7, 82)$ (d) $(25.5, 19)$ and $(28.5, 13)$

2 Television repair charges depend on the time taken for a repair.
Here are some of the charges.

Time in minutes (*T*)	50	80	100	180
Charge in £ (*C*)	35	50	60	100

(a) Sketch a graph of the charge (*C*) against the time (*T*).

(b) Find the equation that links the charge and the time in the form $C = \ldots$

(c) What is the 'call-out charge' (the amount you pay even if no repair is needed)?

(d) Use your equation to work out the charge for a repair that takes $3\frac{1}{2}$ hours.

D Fractional gradient

1 A line has a gradient of $\frac{2}{5}$ and it cuts the y-axis at $(0, 4)$.
Write down the equation of the line.

2 For each of the lines A to F

   (i) find the gradient as a fraction

   (ii) write down the y-intercept

   (iii) write down its equation

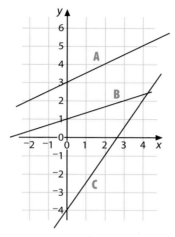 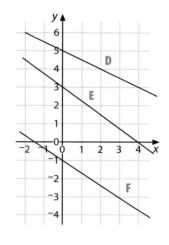

3 Which of these lines is steeper, $y = \frac{1}{2}x - 1$ or $y = \frac{1}{3}x + 5$?

4 Find the equation of the line that passes through

   (a) $(^-5, 0)$ and $(0, 2)$ **(b)** $(0, ^-5)$ and $(3, 0)$ **(c)** $(0, 5)$ and $(6, 0)$

5 (a) Match the equations below to give three pairs of parallel lines.

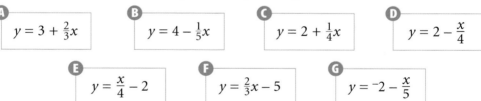

A $y = 3 + \frac{2}{3}x$ **B** $y = 4 - \frac{1}{5}x$ **C** $y = 2 + \frac{1}{4}x$ **D** $y = 2 - \frac{x}{4}$

E $y = \frac{x}{4} - 2$ **F** $y = \frac{2}{3}x - 5$ **G** $y = ^-2 - \frac{x}{5}$

  (b) Which one is the odd one out?

6 The coordinates of three vertices of a square PQRS are
P $(14, ^-10)$, Q $(20, 20)$ and R $(50, 14)$.

Find the equations of the lines QR, PQ and RS.

E Rearranging the equation of a graph

1 Find the gradient of each of these lines.

   (a) $y - x = 4$ **(b)** $y - 2x = 3$ **(c)** $x + y = 7$

   (d) $4x = y - 2$ **(e)** $5x + y = 2$ **(f)** $y + 10 = 3x$

2 Match the equations below to give three pairs of parallel lines.

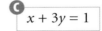

A $y - 2x = 7$ **B** $y + x = 5$ **C** $2x = y - 4$

D $y + 2x = 15$ **E** $y = 3 - 2x$ **F** $y = 8 - x$

3 Find the gradient and y-intercept of each of these lines.

(a) $3y = 9x - 6$ (b) $2y = 4 - 6x$ (c) $4y - 12x = 8$ (d) $2y + 9x = 4$

(e) $5y = x - 10$ (f) $4y = 2x + 3$ (g) $y = 2(x - 5)$ (h) $x = 3y - 9$

4 Which two of these lines are

(a) parallel to the line $y = 3x - 1$

(b) parallel to the line $y = \frac{1}{3}x + 1$

A $3x = y + 2$ **B** $3y = x - 2$

C $x + 3y = 1$ **D** $x - 3y = 5$

E $y + 3x = 2$ **F** $3x - y = 3$

5 Find an equation for the line parallel to $4x + 3y = 1$ through $(^-2, 5)$.
Give the equation in the form $ax + by = c$ where a, b and c are integers.

F Perpendicular lines

1 What is the gradient of any line perpendicular to a line with gradient $\frac{1}{2}$?

2 (a) What is the gradient of any line perpendicular to $y = 4x + 1$?

(b) Find the equation of the line perpendicular to $y = 4x + 1$ that goes through $(0, 7)$.

3 Find the equation of the line
(a) perpendicular to $y = 2x + 4$ through $(0, ^-3)$
(b) perpendicular to $y = 1 - 5x$ through $(0, 6)$
(c) perpendicular to $y = \frac{1}{3}x + 1$ through $(1, 3)$
(d) perpendicular to $y = 9 - \frac{3}{4}x$ through $(^-3, 0)$
(e) perpendicular to $y + x = 8$ through $(2, 4)$

4 Shape PQRS is a rectangle.
Points P and R are on the x-axis.
Point Q is on the y-axis.
The line QR has equation $2y + x = 4$.

(a) Find the coordinates of points Q and R.

(b) Find the equations of the lines PQ, RS and PS.

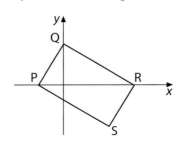

5 Find the equation of the line   (a) perpendicular to $2y - x = 9$ through $(5, 3)$

(b) perpendicular to $3y + 7x = 1$ through $(7, 0)$

(c) perpendicular to $6y - 5x = 2$ through $(5, 2)$

G Line of best fit

1 A small ball was thrown vertically downwards from the top of a high building and its speed was measured at various times during its fall.

The results were plotted and the line of best fit drawn.

(a) Find the gradient of the line of best fit.

(b) Find the vertical intercept.

(c) Write down an approximate equation for the line of best fit.

(d) Use your equation to estimate the speed of the ball after 5 seconds.

(e) What was the initial speed of the ball?

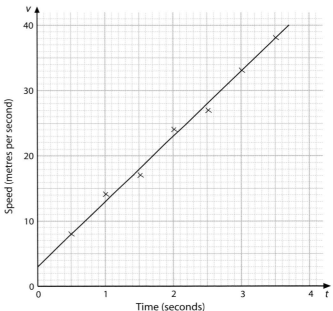

2 Sue dropped a bouncy ball from different heights.
She measured the height of the first bounce each time.
Here are her results.

Height ball dropped from (cm)	30	50	80	100	120
Height of first bounce (cm)	15	32	52	70	81

(a) Plot the points and draw a line of best fit.
Estimate its gradient and y-intercept to one significant figure.
Hence find an approximate equation for your line of best fit.

(b) Use your equation to estimate how high the ball would bounce if dropped from a height of

(i) 65 cm   (ii) 2 m

(c) Which of your estimates will be more reliable?
Why?

Mixed practice 4

You need a pair of compasses.

1 Find the equation of

   (a) line A   **(b)** line B

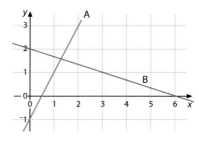

2 Write these numbers using standard form.

   (a) 450 000 000   **(b)** 27 million   **(c)** 0.000 048 3   **(d)** 0.0072

3 Calculate the sides and angles marked with letters.
Give your answers to 1 d.p.

   (a) 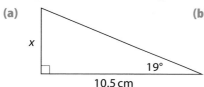   **(b)** 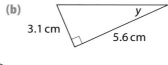   **(c)**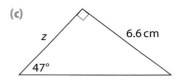

4 Find the gradient and y-intercept of the straight line with equation $2y - 3x = 8$.

5 The sketch shows the position of three radio masts.

   (a) Using a scale of $1 \text{ cm} : 2 \text{ km}$,
draw the diagram accurately.

   (b) Draw accurately the locus of all points
equidistant from

      (i) masts B and R   **(ii)** masts E and R

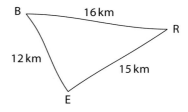

   (c) Mark with an X the position of the point that is equidistant from all three masts.
Write down the distance from each of the masts to X.

6 Write these numbers in ordinary form.

   (a) 2.6×10^5 **(b)** 4.866×10^7 **(c)** 3.66×10^{-2} **(d)** 4.86×10^{-8}

7 A ladder leaning against a vertical wall makes an angle of 68° with the horizontal.
The ladder reaches 4.5 m up the wall.
How far from the wall is the foot of the ladder?

8 A rectangular hall measures 8.4 m by 11 m.
What is the size, in whole centimetres, of the largest square tile that could be used
to tile the hall floor completely without having to cut any tiles?

9 Find an expression for the nth term of the linear sequence 3, 8, 13, 18, 23, …

10 Give the answer to each calculation in standard form correct to two significant figures.

(a) $23\,000^2$ (b) $(7.48 \times 10^8) \times (6.14 \times 10^4)$ (c) $\dfrac{2.47 \times 10^{-4}}{5.31 \times 10^6}$

11 Sally is three times as old as Molly.
Billy is 4 years younger than Molly.
Let x stand for Molly's age in years.

(a) Write expressions in terms of x for Sally's and Billy's ages.

(b) Their three ages add up to 56.
Form an equation in x and solve it to find all their ages.

12 This diagram shows the end wall of a shed.
Calculate the height marked h.

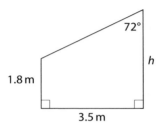

13 Find the equation of

(a) the line parallel to $y = 5x - 3$ going through $(0, 2)$

(b) the line parallel to $x + 2y = 5$ going through $(2, 3)$

(c) the line perpendicular to $y = x + 3$ going through $(1, 1)$

(d) the line perpendicular to $3x + 5y = 2$ that passes through point $(0, 2)$

14 (a) Construct triangle XYZ with $YZ = 6\,cm$, $XZ = 4.5\,cm$ and $XY = 4\,cm$.
Construct the perpendicular from the point X to the line YZ.

(b) Estimate the area of triangle XYZ

15 Fraser has two ordinary dice, numbered 1 to 6.
He throws them both and finds the difference between the two scores.

(a) Find the probability that the difference between the scores is 1.

(b) Find the probability that the difference between the scores is greater than 3.

16 This diagram shows a rectangle ABCD
measuring 70 cm by 40 cm.

Find

(a) the area of triangle ABD

(b) the length BD

(c) the length AH

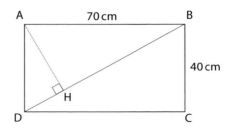

17 A population of 3.76×10^9 is expected to increase by 2.5% each year.
What is the expected population after two years?

18 Karen and Asaan both start with the same number.
Karen halves the number and subtracts it from 14.
Asaan adds 7 to the number, then divides the result by 3.
They end up with the same result.

Find their starting number.

19 Construct triangle PQR with $PQ = 5\,cm$, $QR = 8\,cm$ and $RP = 10\,cm$.
Shade the locus of points in the triangle that are closer to PQ than to QR
and are also closer to Q than to P.

20 This square and rectangle have
the same perimeter.

Form an equation and solve it to find
the dimensions of the rectangle.

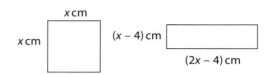

21 Calculate length QR in this diagram.

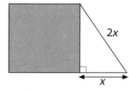

22 Anil's dad is 32 years older than Anil is.
In five years time, Anil's dad will be exactly three times as old as Anil.
How old are Anil and his dad now?

23 Work these out, giving your answers in standard form.

(a) $(4 \times 10^5) + (3 \times 10^3)$ (b) $(5 \times 10^4) \times (2 \times 10^6)$ (c) $\dfrac{6 \times 10^4}{2 \times 10^{-2}}$

24 Write the area of the shaded square
as simply as possible in terms of x.

*25 The members of a club can be either senior or junior.
The ratio of seniors to juniors in the club is $7:9$.
The ratio of males to females in the club is $5:7$.

(a) The club has fewer than 60 members.
How many members does it have?

(b) Which of these fractions is greater?

A   The fraction of club members who are males
B   The fraction of club members who are seniors

(c) One-eighth of the members are senior males.
How many junior females are there?

26 Quadratic expressions and equations

A **Multiplying out expressions such as $(x + 1)(x + 3)$**
C **Multiplying out expressions such as $(x + 1)(x - 3)$ and $(x - 1)(x - 3)$**

1 Multiply out the brackets from each of these and simplify the result.

(a) $(n + 3)(n + 2)$ (b) $(n + 7)(n + 1)$ (c) $(n + 4)^2$

(d) $(n + 6)(n - 1)$ (e) $(n - 3)(n + 9)$ (f) $(n - 1)(n - 2)$

(g) $(x - 5)(x + 2)$ (h) $(x + 2)(x - 6)$ (i) $(x - 3)(x - 5)$

(j) $(x - 1)(x + 1)$ (k) $(x + 10)(x - 10)$ (l) $(x - 9)^2$

2 Find an expression without brackets for the area of each of these rectangles.

(a)
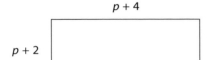

(b)

3 For each statement below, decide whether it is an identity or an equation.
Solve each equation.
Show that each identity is true.

(a) $(n - 3)(n + 8) = n^2 + 13n + 24$

(b) $(n - 8)(n - 4) = n^2 - 12n + 32$

(c) $(n + 5)(n - 2) = n(n + 3) - 10$

(d) $(n + 1)(n + 3) = n(n + 5)$

*4 Find the length of each side in these right-angled triangles.

(a)
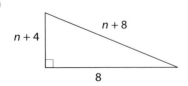

(b)
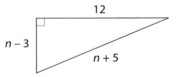

D Factorising quadratic expressions

1 Factorise these expressions.

(a) $n^2 + 7n + 6$ (b) $n^2 + 11n + 24$ (c) $n^2 + 10n + 24$

(d) $n^2 + 9n + 8$ (e) $n^2 + 9n + 18$ (f) $n^2 + 14n + 48$

(g) $n^2 + 14n + 49$ (h) $n^2 + 50n + 49$ (i) $n^2 + 50n + 600$

2 Factorise these.

(a) $n^2 - 5n + 4$ (b) $n^2 + 6n - 7$ (c) $n^2 - 2n - 3$

(d) $n^2 + 3n - 4$ (e) $n^2 - 9n + 8$ (f) $n^2 + 4n - 12$

(g) $x^2 - 9x + 20$ (h) $x^2 - 6x - 7$ (i) $x^2 - 2x - 24$

(j) $x^2 - 10x + 21$ (k) $x^2 + 6x - 16$ (l) $x^2 - 7x + 10$

(m) $x^2 - 4x + 4$ (n) $x^2 - 12x + 36$ (o) $x^2 - 18x + 81$

3 Factorise these.

(a) $x^2 - 81$ (b) $y^2 - 36$ (c) $n^2 - 121$

4 (a) Factorise $n^2 - 9$.

(b) Use your answer to find the value of each of these.

     (i) $7^2 - 9$ (ii) $13^2 - 9$ (iii) $97^2 - 9$

5 (a) Factorise $n^2 + 5n + 6$.

(b) Hence show that $n^2 + 5n + 6$ must be even for any integer n.

6 The nth term of a sequence is $n^2 + 6n + 9$.

(a) Work out the first five terms of the sequence.

(b) Show that every term in the infinite sequence must be a square number.

7 (a) Factorise $n^2 + 9n + 20$.

(b) Hence find the value of $n^2 + 9n + 20$ when

     (i) $n = 5$ (ii) $n = {}^-4$ (iii) $n = {}^-5$

E Solving quadratic equations

1 Solve these equations.

(a) $x^2 - 5x + 6 = 0$ (b) $x^2 - 7x = 0$ (c) $x^2 - x - 30 = 0$

(d) $x^2 + 7x = 0$ (e) $x^2 + 10x + 21 = 0$ (f) $x^2 + 8x + 15 = 0$

(g) $x^2 - 10x + 24 = 0$ (h) $x^2 - 3x - 4 = 0$ (i) $x^2 + 2x - 8 = 0$

(j) $x^2 + 9x + 20 = 0$ (k) $x^2 - x - 20 = 0$ (l) $x^2 - 9x + 20 = 0$

2 Solve these equations.

(a) $x^2 + 6x + 10 = 2$ (b) $x^2 + 6x + 3 = 2x$ (c) $x^2 + 9x + 21 = 3$

(d) $x^2 + 18 = 9x$ (e) $x^2 - 12x + 80 = 48$ (f) $x^2 + 15x + 30 = 3x - 2$

(g) $x^2 = 12x - 20$ (h) $x^2 - 10x = {}^-16$ (i) $x(x - 3) = 10$

(j) $x(x - 4) = 5$ (k) $(x - 3)(x + 1) = {}^-3$ (l) $(x + 5)(x - 1) = 7$

F Graphs and the solutions of quadratic equations

1 (a) Factorise each expression.

(i) $x^2 + 8x + 15$ **(ii)** $x^2 - 8x + 15$ **(iii)** $x^2 - 10x + 24$

(b) Use your answers to part (a) to match each equation below to its graph.

P $\quad y = x^2 + 8x + 15$

Q $\quad y = x^2 - 8x + 15$

R $\quad y = x^2 - 10x + 24$

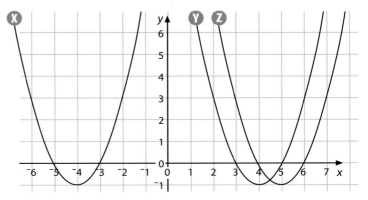

2 For each of these equations, find the values of x where its graph crosses the x-axis.

(a) $y = x^2 + 5x + 4$ **(b)** $y = x^2 - 7x$

(c) $y = x^2 - 10x + 16$ **(d)** $y = x^2 - 3x - 4$

(e) $y = x^2 - 4$ **(f)** $y = x^2 + x - 12$

3 The diagram shows two congruent parabolas.
One is the graph of $y = x^2$.

Which of these is the equation
of the other parabola?

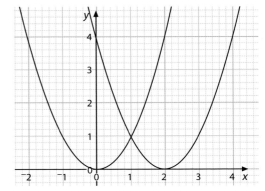

P $\quad y = x^2 + 4x + 4$ **Q** $\quad y = x^2 - 4x + 4$

R $\quad y = x^2 + 2x + 4$ **S** $\quad y = x^2 - 2x + 4$

4 Make a sketch of the graph of each equation below.
Show clearly the coordinates of the points where each graph crosses the x- and y-axes.

(a) $y = x^2 + 6x + 5$ **(b)** $y = x^2 + 3x$

(c) $y = x^2 - 7x + 10$ **(d)** $y = x^2 - 14x + 49$

(e) $y = x^2 - 6x - 7$ **(f)** $y = x^2 - 25$

G Solving problems

1 The area of this rectangle is $63\,\text{cm}^2$.

$(x + 5)\,\text{cm}$

$(x + 3)\,\text{cm}$

  (a) Form an equation, in terms of x, and show that
it can be written as $x^2 + 8x - 48 = 0$.

  (b) Solve the equation $x^2 + 8x - 48 = 0$ and
find the length and width of the rectangle.

2 The area of the square is twice the area of the rectangle.

$x\,\text{cm}$

$x\,\text{cm}$

$(x + 3)\,\text{cm}$

$2\,\text{cm}$

  (a) Form an equation in x and show that it can be simplified to $x^2 - 4x - 12 = 0$.

  (b) Solve the equation $x^2 - 4x - 12 = 0$ and find the perimeter of the square.

3 The area of this path is $36\,\text{m}^2$.

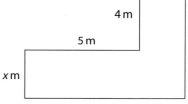

$x\,\text{m}$

$4\,\text{m}$

$5\,\text{m}$

$x\,\text{m}$

  (a) Form an equation in terms of x.

  (b) Show that the equation can be simplified
to $x^2 + 9x - 36 = 0$.

  (c) Solve the equation to find x, the width of the path.

4 The width of a rectangle is $5\,\text{cm}$ less than the length of the rectangle.
The area of the rectangle is $300\,\text{cm}^2$.

  (a) What is the length of the rectangle?

  (b) What is the perimeter of the rectangle?

*5 Find the length of each side of this right-angled triangle.

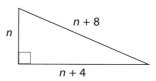

n

$n + 8$

$n + 4$

*6 The expression for the nth term of a sequence is $n^2 + 3n - 5$.

  (a) What is the 5th term of the sequence?

  (b) Which term of the sequence is 265?

27 Handling secondary data

A Drawing conclusions from data

This table gives information about the estimated costs of road accidents in Scotland.

Total estimated accident costs in Scotland (£ million) at 2004 prices, by severity
Years: 1994 to 2004

| Year | Accidents involving injury | | | | Accidents involving damage only | All accidents |
	Fatal	Serious	Slight	Total		
1994	537.6	820.3	213.1	1571.0	396.1	1967.1
1995	605.4	769.8	213.9	1589.1	389.5	1978.6
1996	519.8	638.7	222.9	1381.4	377.7	1759.2
1997	555.4	633.7	234.0	1423.1	389.5	1812.6
1998	564.5	639.4	231.5	1435.4	385.7	1821.1
1999	450.1	600.1	217.1	1267.4	359.6	1627.0
2000	476.9	561.9	215.4	1254.2	352.4	1606.6
2001	508.4	535.6	209.7	1253.7	342.4	1596.1
2002	448.0	502.9	205.6	1156.6	333.2	1489.8
2003	482.8	463.6	201.0	1147.4	321.7	1469.1
2004	447.0	429.9	201.9	1078.8	320.2	1399.0

Source: Scottish Executive, Road Accidents Scotland 2004

1 Why are the costs all given 'at 2004 prices'?

2 (a) What was the estimated cost, in £, of all accidents in 2004?

(b) Find the percentage reduction in the estimated cost of all accidents between 1994 and 2004.

3 (a) By looking at the table, decide which type of accident had the greatest percentage reduction in costs between 1994 and 2004.

(b) Calculate this percentage reduction.

The table below shows the average number of accidents per year in Scotland over the period 2000–2004, broken down by vehicle type. (Source as above)

Vehicle type	Pedal cycle	Motor cycle	Car	Taxi	Minibus	Bus/ coach	Light goods	Heavy goods	Other
Average accidents	865	1146	18 285	521	114	1089	908	931	397

4 A reporter draws the conclusion from this data that a car is the most dangerous type of vehicle to travel in.

Is this conclusion justified? Explain the reasons for your answer.

This map shows the London area divided into Inner London and Outer London.

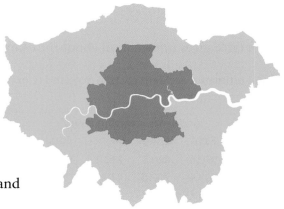

The tables below give information about the area and population of Inner and Outer London.

The population data is taken from the 2001 Census.

Population and area of London

| | Population (thousands) | | | |
	Males	Females	Total	Area in km²
Inner London	1340.6	1425.5	2766.1	319
Outer London	2128.2	2277.8	4406.0	1253
Total	3468.8	3703.3	7172.1	1572

Population of London, by age group

| | Population (thousands) in age groups | | | | | |
	0–19	20–39	40–59	60–79	80+	Total
Inner London	663.2	1142.4	579.3	309.0	72.2	2766.1
Outer London	1119.0	1410.7	1083.0	627.3	166.0	4406.0
Total	1782.2	2553.1	1662.3	936.3	238.2	7172.1

1 What percentage of the population of Outer London are female?

2 What percentage of the population of London live in Inner London?

3 Calculate the population density of Inner and Outer London in thousands of people per km².
Write a sentence comparing the two.

4 (a) Make a table showing the percentage of the population in each age group in Inner London and in Outer London.

(b) Write a short report comparing the two age distributions.

The answers to questions 3 and 4 suggest that there may be a link between the percentage of people aged 60 or over and population density.

This may be investigated further by looking at the data for the individual boroughs that make up Inner and Outer London.

Inner London	Population (000)		Area (km²)
	60+	Total	
Camden	28.1	198.0	22
City of London	1.3	7.2	3
Hackney	25.6	202.8	19
Hammersmith & Fulham	17.3	165.2	16
Haringey	29.0	216.5	30
Islington	24.1	175.8	15
Kensington and Chelsea	26.4	158.9	12
Lambeth	33.1	266.2	27
Lewisham	36.2	248.9	35
Newham	29.9	243.9	36
Southwark	33.7	244.9	29
Tower Hamlets	24.7	196.1	20
Wandsworth	35.9	260.4	34
Westminster	29.7	181.3	21

Outer London	Population (000)		Area (km²)
	60+	Total	
Barking and Dagenham	30.3	163.9	36
Barnet	58.3	314.6	87
Bexley	45.0	218.3	61
Brent	41.4	263.5	43
Bromley	63.7	295.5	150
Croydon	56.3	330.6	87
Ealing	46.9	300.9	56
Enfield	49.8	273.6	81
Greenwich	36.2	214.4	47
Harrow	39.4	206.8	50
Havering	50.8	224.2	112
Hillingdon	44.3	243.0	116
Hounslow	32.8	212.3	56
Kingston-upon-Thames	25.2	147.3	37
Merton	31.5	187.9	38
Redbridge	43.4	238.6	56
Richmond-upon-Thames	30.4	172.3	57
Sutton	33.7	179.8	44
Waltham Forest	33.9	218.3	39

 5 (This question is most easily done on a spreadsheet by entering all the data, without names, into three columns.)

	A	B	C
1	28.1	198.0	22
2	1.3	7.2	3
3	25.6	202.8	19

(a) For each borough calculate

(i) the population density in thousands of people per km²

(ii) the percentage of people aged 60 or over

(b) Draw a scatter diagram with population density on the horizontal axis and percentage aged 60+ on the vertical axis.

(c) What conclusion do you draw from the scatter diagram?

(d) There is one borough that is outside the general pattern of the rest. Which borough is this?

28 Solving inequalities

A Review: writing and interpreting inequalities

1 Copy and complete the following by replacing ▪ by the correct symbol, < or >.

   (a) 3 ▪ π **(b)** 7 ▪ $\sqrt{7}$ **(c)** 4^2 ▪ 9 **(d)** 3 ▪ $\sqrt{10}$

2 Write an inequality, using x, for each diagram.

   (a) 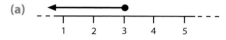   **(b)**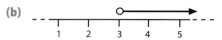

   (c)    **(d)**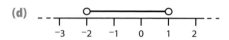

3 Draw number lines to show these inequalities.

   (a) $n \le 2$ **(b)** $n > {}^{-}2$ **(c)** $4 \le n \le 6$ **(d)** ${}^{-}3 < n < 4$

4 List all the **integers** satisfied by these inequalities.

   (a) $0 \le n < 6$ **(b)** $2 \le n \le 5$ **(c)** ${}^{-}1 < n \le 2$ **(d)** ${}^{-}4 < n < 5$

5 Write down all the integers n such that $n^2 \le 4$.

6 **(a)** Given that a stands for the size of an angle in degrees, write an inequality for each of these statements.

     (i) The angle is less than 90°.   **(ii)** The angle is greater than 180°.

   (b) What is the special name given to the angles in each case?

7 Given that w stands for the weight of a letter in grams, write an inequality for the statement 'The letter weighs 60 g or less.'

B Manipulating inequalities
C Solving simple inequalities

1 Which of the following are equivalent to $n \ge 7$?

   A $n + 1 \ge 6$ **B** $2n \ge 14$ **C** $7 \le n$ **D** $\dfrac{n}{2} \ge 3\tfrac{1}{2}$ **E** $n + 4 \ge 11$

2 Which of the following are equivalent to $p < 6$?

   A $p - 5 < 1$ **B** $2p < 8$ **C** $5p < 30$ **D** $\dfrac{p}{2} < 12$ **E** $p + 3 < 3$

3 Find the four equivalent pairs in these inequalities.

| $3x \geq 9$ | $x + 4 \leq 6$ | $x \geq 2$ | $\frac{x}{3} \leq 1$ | $x - 1 \geq 1$ | $3 \leq x$ | $x \leq 3$ | $x \leq 2$ |

4 Solve these inequalities.

(a) $n + 2 \leq 10$ (b) $m - 1 \geq 9$ (c) $2g \leq 12$ (d) $\frac{h}{3} < 4$

(e) $3x \geq {}^-18$ (f) $4y > 14$ (g) $w + 3 < 7\frac{1}{2}$ (h) $\frac{p}{2} \leq 5\frac{1}{2}$

5 Solve $5x + 2 \geq 27$.
Show the solution set on a number line.

6 Solve each of these inequalities.

(a) $3w + 5 \geq 20$ (b) $5x - 2 \leq 18$ (c) $3 + 4y > 19$ (d) $2z - 1 \leq 10$

(e) $x + 8 < 1$ (f) $h - 5 > {}^-3$ (g) $t - 1 \leq {}^-4$ (h) $5n + 11 \geq 1$

(i) $3k - 8 > {}^-2$ (j) $2f + 3 > {}^-5$ (k) $6x + 5 < 14$ (l) $2b + 9 \leq 1$

(m) $4k - 9 > {}^-1$ (n) $3v - 4 \leq {}^-1$ (o) $5n + 3 \geq 10$ (p) $4h + 1 \geq {}^-5$

7 Solve each of these inequalities.

(a) $3(w + 5) \geq 21$ (b) $5(x - 2) < 10$ (c) $4(y - 3) > 2$ (d) $2(3x + 1) \leq 8$

8 Solve each of these inequalities.

(a) $\frac{b}{3} + 1 < 5$ (b) $\frac{a}{4} - 2 \geq 5$ (c) $\frac{x}{2} + 6 < 4$ (d) $\frac{n}{8} + 4 \leq 3$

(e) $\frac{k + 3}{2} \geq 5$ (f) $\frac{p - 1}{4} < 7$ (g) $\frac{h + 8}{3} > 4$ (h) $\frac{m + 9}{5} \leq 1$

D Unknown on both sides
E Multiplying or dividing by a negative number

1 Solve each of these inequalities.

(a) $3x < x + 8$ (b) $6y > y + 10$ (c) $3z + 1 \geq z + 9$

(d) $5m + 3 < 2m + 15$ (e) $5n - 3 \leq 4n$ (f) $7p + 5 > 5p + 10$

(g) $3q - 3 \leq 2q + 1$ (h) $8w - 3 < 7 + 3w$ (i) $6k - 3 \geq 2k + 3$

(j) $7g - 9 > 4g + 15$ (k) $2h + 3 \leq h + 1$ (l) $4b - 7 \leq 3b - 1$

(m) $5c - 9 > 3c - 2$ (n) $6d + 2 < d - 3$ (o) $3a + 6 \geq a + 1$

2 Solve each of these.

(a) $3(x + 1) \geq 15 + x$ (b) $4(y + 2) \leq 3y + 10$ (c) $3(z + 4) \geq z + 14$

(d) $4(m - 3) < 2(m + 3)$ (e) $5(n - 2) \leq 2(n + 1)$ (f) $6(p - 5) > 3(p - 7)$

3 Solve each of these.

(a) $3q + 8 \geq 5q$

(b) $9 + 7w < 10w$

(c) $2(k + 3) > 3k$

(d) $3m + 7 \geq m + 1$

(e) $3(h + 3) \leq 7h + 1$

(f) $9 + 2a \leq 5a - 3$

(g) $b + 1 \leq 6b - 19$

(h) $2c < 5c - 12$

(i) $d - 1 < 4d - 10$

(j) $2k + 7 < 7k + 3$

(k) $p + 1 \leq 6p + 16$

(l) $5x - 1 > 3(x + 2)$

4 Solve each of these.

(a) $\dfrac{n + 9}{4} < n$

(b) $\dfrac{n + 11}{2} \geq 6 + n$

(c) $\dfrac{n + 1}{3} > n - 5$

(d) $\dfrac{4 + n}{2} > \dfrac{15 + n}{4}$

(e) $\dfrac{3n - 1}{5} > \dfrac{n + 1}{2}$

(f) $\dfrac{2n + 1}{2} \leq \dfrac{4n - 1}{3}$

5 Solve each of these inequalities.

(a) $^-2x > ^-6$

(b) $^-3t \leq 12$

(c) $^-4r \geq ^-6$

(d) $4 < 9 - p$

(e) $9 \leq 15 - 3d$

(f) $1 + f < 19 - 5f$

(g) $5n - 3 \leq 18 - 2n$

(h) $22 - 4w \geq 3w + 8$

(i) $5 - 2z > 14 - 5z$

(j) $2(x + 5) > 4 - x$

(k) $11 - 5m \leq 3(m + 1)$

(l) $6(k + 1) < 2(5 - 2k)$

6 Solve each of these.

(a) $\dfrac{n - 3}{2} \geq 6 - n$

(b) $\dfrac{5 - n}{3} > \dfrac{6 - n}{2}$

(c) $\dfrac{4 - n}{2} \leq \dfrac{2 - 5n}{4}$

F Combined inequalities

1 Solve the inequality $1 < 2x - 3 \leq 15$ and show the solution set on a number line.

2 Solve these inequalities.

(a) $8 \leq n + 5 < 12$

(b) $6 < 2n < 14$

(c) $1 < n - 3 \leq 2$

(d) $10 \leq 5n \leq 20$

(e) $2 < \dfrac{n}{2} < 4$

(f) $^-1 \leq n - 5 < 4$

(g) $^-5 \leq x - 4 < 5$

(h) $5 < 2x \leq 10$

(i) $7 \leq 2x + 1 < 13$

(j) $2 < 3x - 1 < 11$

(k) $4 < 5x - 6 \leq 9$

(l) $1 \leq 4x + 5 \leq 15$

3 (a) Solve $11 \leq 2x + 3 < 17$.

(b) List the values of x, where x is an **integer**, such that $11 \leq 2x + 3 < 17$.

4 List the values of n, where n is an integer, such that

(a) $6 \leq 2n \leq 16$

(b) $8 \leq n + 2 < 13$

(c) $7 < \dfrac{n}{3} < 9$

(d) $1 \leq 3n + 1 \leq 13$

(e) $5 < 4x - 3 \leq 13$

(f) $0 < 2x - 7 < 8$

5 Solve the inequality $^-1 \leq \dfrac{4x + 1}{3} < 7$.

*6 List five integers that satisfy the inequality $5 < 2n^2 + 3 \leq 60$.

29 Simultaneous equations

B Solving equations 1

1 Solve the following pairs of simultaneous equations to find the values of x and y.

(a) $7x + y = 17$
$3x + y = 9$

(b) $2x + 4y = 14$
$2x + 3y = 11$

(c) $5x + 3y = 29$
$5x + 6y = 38$

(d) $x + 2y = 5$
$4x + 3y = 15$

(e) $5x + 4y = 30$
$3x + 2y = 16$

(f) $x + 4y = 26$
$3x + 5y = 36$

(g) $2x + 3y = 8$
$3x + 2y = 7$

(h) $4x + 7y = 33$
$5x + 3y = 24$

(i) $7x + 5y = 54$
$5x + 2y = 37$

2 Solve each pair of simultaneous equations.

(a) $2x + 3y = 12$
$2x + y = 6$

(b) $2a + b = 7$
$5a + b = 19$

(c) $4m + 7n = 27$
$2n + 4m = 2$

(d) $2h + 5k = 1$
$h + 2k = 1$

(e) $2p + q = 4$
$11p + 4q = 25$

(f) $6c + 3d = 18$
$6d + 4c = 16$

(g) $4u + 3v = 10$
$3u + 4v = 4$

(h) $3w + 7z = 18$
$5w + 3z = 17$

(i) $3f + 2g = 9$
$7g + 8f = 19$

C Forming and solving equations

1 The cost of 5 cheese sandwiches and 4 ham sandwiches is £15.50.
The cost of 5 cheese sandwiches and 2 ham sandwiches is £11.50.

(a) Which of these pairs of equations is correct for the statements above?

A
$c + 4h = 1550$
$c + 2h = 1150$

B
$5c + 4h = 1550$
$5c + 2h = 1150$

C
$5c + 4h = 1150$
$5c + 2h = 1550$

(b) Solve the correct pair of simultaneous equations to find the cost of
a cheese sandwich and the cost of a ham sandwich.

2 Helen and Greg buy some gel pens and some coloured pencils.
Helen spends £3.35 on 3 gel pens and 5 coloured pencils.
Greg spends £7.05 on 9 gel pens and 3 coloured pencils.

With the cost of a gel pen g pence and the cost of a coloured pencil c pence, form two
equations and solve them to find the cost of a gel pen and the cost of a coloured pencil.

3 3 bags of jelly beans and 2 bags of chocolate raisins weigh 670 g.
5 bags of jelly beans and 3 bags of chocolate raisins weigh 1070 g.

Find the weight of a bag of jelly beans and the weight of a bag of chocolate raisins.

4 In a park there are some dogs and their owners.
Altogether they have 35 heads and 110 legs.
How many dogs are there in the park?

5 A bag contains a mixture of £1 and 50p coins.
There are 100 coins in the bag and their total value is £82.
How many of each type of coin are there?

D Solving equations 2
E Substitution

1 Solve each pair of simultaneous equations.

(a) $x + y = 16$
$x - y = 4$

(b) $2x - 5y = 1$
$2x + 5y = 11$

(c) $3x - 7y = 7$
$7y + 2x = 28$

(d) $2x + y = 11$
$5x - 3y = 11$

(e) $5x + 6y = 37$
$x - y = 3$

(f) $3x - 4y = 3$
$2y + 5x = 31$

(g) $x - 2y = 2$
$4x + 3y = 41$

(h) $2x + 5y = 33$
$3x - 2y = 2$

(i) $x - 3y = 8$
$3x + 8y = 92$

2 Solve each pair of simultaneous equations.

(a) $x + 2y = 8$
$x - 2y = 2$

(b) $3x - y = 5$
$4x + y = 2$

(c) $5x - 3y = 6$
$3y + x = 3$

(d) $2x - y = 34$
$x + 3y = 3$

(e) $3x + y = 5$
$7x - 4y = 18$

(f) $5x - 6y = {}^-17$
$3x + 2y = 1$

(g) $2x - 4y = 1$
$3x + 5y = 18$

(h) $x + 3y = 1$
$4x - 2y = 11$

(i) $x - 2y = 5$
$5y + x = {}^-23$

3 Solve each pair of simultaneous equations.

(a) $3x - y = 13$
$x - y = 3$

(b) $2h - k = 6$
$3h - 4k = 4$

(c) $4a - 5b = 3$
$3a - b = 5$

(d) $m - 2n = 5$
$6m - 3n = 18$

(e) $2p - 3q = 0$
$3p - 4q = 1$

(f) $4u - 2v = {}^-2$
$5u - 9v = 4$

4 The sum of two numbers is 42 and the difference between them is 18.
Given that a is the larger number and b is the smaller number, find a and b.

5 Solve each pair of simultaneous equations.

(a) $y = 3x - 1$
$2x + y = 19$

(b) $2y - 5x = 3$
$y = 9 - 5x$

(c) $3y = 2 + 4x$
$y + 2x = 9$

(d) $6y - x = 1$
$y = \frac{1}{3}x$

(e) $y = 2x - 9$
$2y - x = {}^-15$

(f) $5x - y = 15$
$y = 3 - 4x$

F Graphs and simultaneous equations

1 Use the graphs to solve each pair of simultaneous equations.

(a) $x + y = 10$
$y - 2x = 1$

(b) $2x + 5y = 17$
$y - 2x = 1$

(c) $x + y = 10$
$2x + 5y = 17$

Check each solution by substituting into the equations.

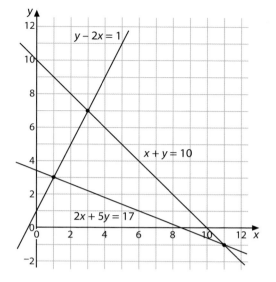

2 What are the coordinates of the point where the lines $y + x = 10$ and $y - x = 5$ intersect?

3 Graphs of $2x - 5y = 1$ and $x + 5y = 4$ are shown below.

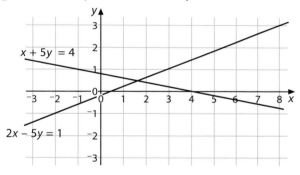

(a) Estimate by eye where the graphs intersect.

(b) Use algebra to find the exact coordinates of the intersection point.

4 Where do the lines $y = 3x - 6$ and $y = 9 - 2x$ intersect?

5 Show that there is no solution to the simultaneous equations

$y - 4x = 1$
$2y = 8x + 3$

6 Show that there are infinitely many solutions to the simultaneous equations

$y = \frac{1}{4}x + 3$
$4y - x = 12$

G Mixed questions

1 Solve each pair of simultaneous equations.
  Give any non-integer solutions as fractions.

  (a) $6x + 5y = 28$
       $5x - y = 13$

  (b) $2a + 7b = 26$
       $2b + 5a = 3$

  (c) $3h - 4k = 17$
       $4h + 5k = 2$

  (d) $2m - 3n = 5$
       $6m - n = 3$

  (e) $3p - 4q = 2$
       $p = 1 - 2q$

  (f) $y = 3x - 5$
       $y = 2x + 6$

Solve each of the following problems by forming and solving a pair of simultaneous equations.

2 Two apples and three bananas cost 85p.
  Five apples and a banana cost £1.15.
  What is the cost of a banana?

3 Amy bought 6 kg of potatoes for £5.08.
  Some of the potatoes were red and some white.
  The red potatoes cost 90p per kg and the white potatoes cost 80p per kg.

  How many kilograms of each kind of potatoes did she buy?

4 The picture shows a trellis made from 7 m of timber.
  The perimeter of the trellis is 3.2 m.

  What are the dimensions of the trellis?

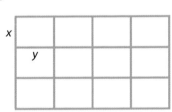

5 A country show lasted three days.
  The entrance fee on the first two days was £5 and it was reduced to £3 for the final day.
  8400 people attended the show.
  £37 000 was paid in entrance fees over the three days.

  How many people attended on the final day?

6 The mean of two numbers is 51.
  The difference between them is 36.

  Find the two numbers.

7 The cost of entry to a football match was £15 and £12.
  1000 more people paid the higher price than the lower price.
  £244 500 was paid for tickets.

  How many people attended the match?

Newchester United
North and South Stands: £15
East and West Stands: £12

*8 A fraction has a value of $\frac{1}{2}$ when 1 is added to the numerator.
   The fraction's value is $\frac{1}{3}$ when 1 is added to the denominator.
   Find the fraction.

30 Sine and cosine

A Finding the adjacent or opposite side from the hypotenuse and angle

1 For each side marked **?**, state whether it is opposite or adjacent to
the given angle and find its length, to one decimal place.

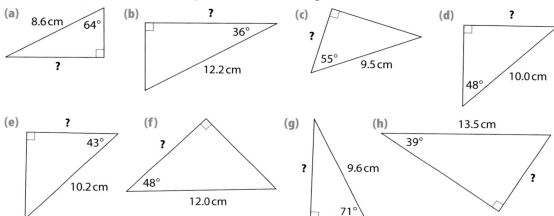

B Finding the hypotenuse from another side and an angle

1 In each triangle find the length of the hypotenuse to 1 d.p.
Decide carefully whether to use sine or cosine.

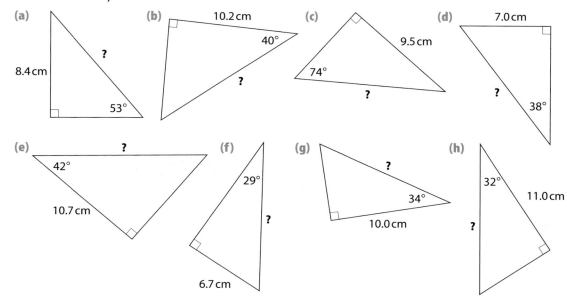

C Finding an angle

1 Find each angle marked by a letter by choosing a calculation from one of the boxes then doing it as a key sequence on your calculator.

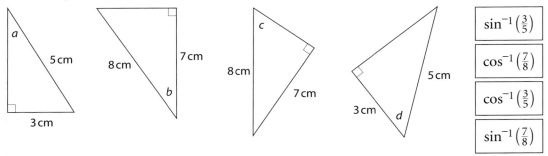

$$\sin^{-1}\left(\tfrac{3}{5}\right)$$

$$\cos^{-1}\left(\tfrac{7}{8}\right)$$

$$\cos^{-1}\left(\tfrac{3}{5}\right)$$

$$\sin^{-1}\left(\tfrac{7}{8}\right)$$

2 Find the marked angles, giving your answers to 1 d.p.

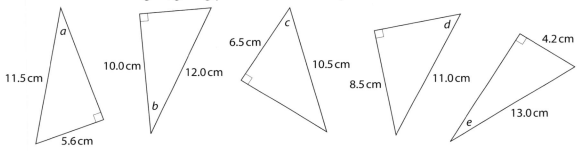

D Mixed questions, including tangent and Pythagoras

1 Find the angle or length marked x in each triangle, to 1 d.p.

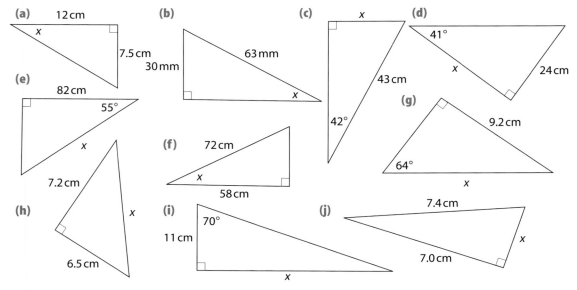

2 ABCD is a design for a children's slide.
BD is 136 cm and DC is 195 cm.

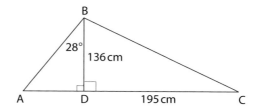

(a) Calculate angle BCD.

(b) Angle ABD is 28°.
Calculate the distance AB.

3 The angle of elevation of a kite is shown
from two positions, Q and R.
PQ = 70 m.

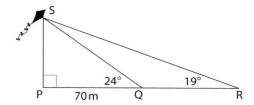

(a) Calculate PS, the height of the kite.

(b) Calculate the length RS.

4 Starting from a tree, a slug slides 20 metres north to a flower pot.
It then slithers 13 metres west to a cabbage.
Finally it crawls straight back to the tree.

Draw a sketch and calculate these.

(a) The length of the return journey from the cabbage to the tree

(b) The bearing of the return journey

5 The height of a yacht's mast BE is 8 m.
Calculate length AD.

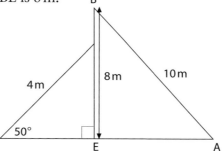

6 The diagram shows a trapezium.
PQ is parallel to SR.
Angle P = 90°.
PQ = 12 cm, PS = 5 cm and RS = 9 cm.

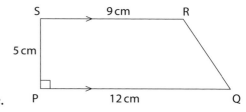

(a) Calculate the size of angle Q.
Give your answer correct to one decimal place.

(b) Calculate the size of angle R.

(c) Calculate the length of QR, correct to one decimal place.

*7 A dodecagon is drawn by spacing 12 dots equally around a circle and
then joining them with straight lines.
The perimeter of the decagon is 50 cm.
Calculate the radius of the circle to the nearest 0.1 cm.

Mixed practice 5

1 Multiply out each expression and write the result in its simplest form.

   (a) $(x + 2)(x + 3)$ (b) $(x + 3)^2$ (c) $(x + 5)(x - 3)$ (d) $(x - 4)(x - 5)$

2 One day, Jane asked all 147 students in her year
   what kind of lunch they had had.
   The table shows the results of her survey.

	Girls	Boys
Hot lunch	15	31
Cold lunch	35	40
No lunch	12	14

   (a) What percentage of Jane's year are girls?

   (b) What percentage of the boys had a hot lunch?

   (c) What percentage of those who had no lunch were girls?

3 Solve these inequalities.

   (a) $2x - 9 \leq 1$ (b) $3x + 13 > 4$ (c) $3x + 4 < 7x - 6$ (d) $4(x + 1) \geq 14 - x$

4 Two groups of people went to a cinema.
   The first group consisted of 3 adults and 5 children and paid £26.
   The second group consisted of 2 adults and 6 children and paid £24.

   By setting up and solving a pair of simultaneous equations, calculate the cost
   of an adult ticket and the cost of a child ticket.

5 The diagram shows trapezium ABCD.
   Give all answers correct to 1 d.p.

   (a) Calculate length PD.

   (b) Calculate length AP.

   (c) Find the perimeter of the trapezium.

   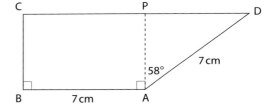

6 Factorise these.

   (a) $x^2 - 49$ (b) $x^2 + 8x + 15$ (c) $x^2 + 4x - 12$ (d) $x^2 - 7x - 18$

7 From a point P, 20 metres away on horizontal ground from a vertical building,
   the angle of elevation of X, the top of the building, is 34°.

   (a) How high is the building?

   (b) A cable is to go from point X to point P.
        How long will the cable be?

   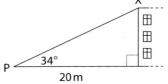

8 Solve $7 \leq 2x - 3 < 11$.

9 Solve each pair of simultaneous equations.

   (a) $2x + y = 13$ (b) $3x + 2y = 8$ (c) $3x + 2y = 2$
        $4x - y = 17$ $4x + 3y = 10$ $2x - 3y = {^-}16$

10 Solve these equations.

(a) $x^2 + 3x + 2 = 0$ (b) $x^2 - 5x - 6 = 0$ (c) $x^2 - 8x + 15 = 0$

11 (a) Calculate the angle ABC in this diagram.

(b) Find the area of triangle ABC, correct to 3 s.f.

12 List all the integers n such that $n^2 < 4$.

13 At what point do the lines with equations $2x - y = 0$ and $y = 3x - 1$ intersect?

14 Solve these equations.

(a) $x^2 - x = 0$ (b) $x^2 - x = 6$ (c) $x^2 = 5x - 6$

15 Solve these inequalities.

(a) $\frac{x}{2} + 3 \geq 7$ (b) $\frac{x+3}{2} > 7$ (c) $\frac{x-1}{5} \leq x$ (d) $\frac{2x+3}{5} \leq x + 1$

16 (a) Find the prime factorisation of 60 and write it using index notation.

(b) Use prime factorisation to find the lowest common multiple of 60 and 48.

(c) Use prime factorisation to find the highest common factor of 60 and 105.

17 The area of this rectangle is $48\,\text{cm}^2$.

(a) Show that x satisfies the equation
$x^2 + 4x - 60 = 0$.

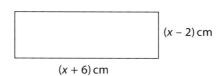

(b) Solve the equation to find x.

(c) Write down the dimensions of the rectangle.

18 Solve this pair of simultaneous equations.

$4x + y = 20$
$2y = x + 4$

19 Simplify each of these expressions as far as possible.

(a) $p(1 - q) - q(1 - p)$ (b) $x(3 - y^2) + 4xy(x^2 - y)$ (c) $a^2(b + 3c) - c(a^2 - 2b)$

20 PQRS is a trapezium with PS parallel to QR.
Angles PQS and QRS are both right angles.
PS $= 20\,\text{cm}$ and $\sin a = 0.4$.

(a) Calculate QS.

(b) Write down the value of $\cos b$.

(c) Calculate QR.

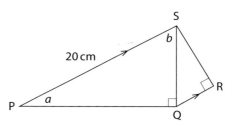

21 Solve the equation $(x-4)(x-5) = 2(x-2)$.

22 List the integer values of n that satisfy the inequality $^-1 \le \dfrac{3n+1}{2} < 4$.

23 Sketch the graph of $y = x^2 - 7x - 8$.
Mark clearly the coordinates where the graph cuts the x- and y-axes.

24 (a) An open box consisting of four sides and a base
is made of mahogany with a thickness of 12 mm.

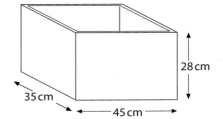

    (i) Find the volume of the mahogany used
to make the box.

    (ii) The density of mahogany is 0.85 g/cm³.
What is the mass of the box in kg?

(b) A box with the same dimensions is made of a different wood.
This box has a mass of 5.06 kg. What is the density of this wood?

*25 Jawal has two beakers, A and B.
Beaker A contains 40 ml water and beaker B contains 30 ml water.
Jawal pours some water from B into A. Afterwards, beaker A contains
three times as much water as beaker B.

Calculate how much water was poured from B into A, showing your working.

*26 Elaine has a journey to make.
If she travels at an average speed of 40 m.p.h. it will take 6 hours less
than if she travels at an average speed of 25 m.p.h.
How long will the journey take if she travels at 50 m.p.h.?

*27 An insect at A wants to crawl across the surface of
the cuboid to the opposite vertex B.

The blue lines show some possible routes.

What is the length of the shortest route from
A to B on the surface of the cuboid?

Explain why your route must be the shortest.

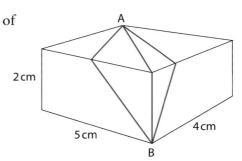

*28 An engineer has three pumps, A, B and C.
Pumps A and B working together will empty a 1000-litre tank in 3 minutes.
Pumps B and C will do it in 4 minutes.
Pumps A and C will do it in 6 minutes.

How long will it take to empty the tank if all three pumps are used?

*29 The number 104 000 000 has six terminal zeros.
How many terminal zeros are there in the result of $1 \times 2 \times 3 \times 4 \times \ldots \times 98 \times 99 \times 100$?